Roadside With
LONDON'S COUNTRY BUSES & GREEN LINE COACHES

Jim Blake

Visions International Entertainment Ltd

It is hard to believe that this picture, in the yard of Chelsham Garage, was taken as late as 1st May 1976, since aside from the RF having had its "bullseye" filler cap painted over and a London Country fleet name, it could have been taken up to twenty-five years earlier! Chelsham was the last major operator of RTs, used on the busy 403 but replaced by RMCs shortly after this picture was taken. The buses here are RF69, RT986 and RT3461 (CM). The latter was one of three that survived here to be painted in corporate N.B.C. livery a year later, and was subsequently preserved. The other RTs visible on the left are withdrawn in a field behind the garage.

Roadside With
LONDON'S COUNTRY BUSES
& GREEN LINE COACHES

Published by Visions International Entertainment Limited

ISBN: 978-1-9126952-5-6

© 2019 Jim Blake and Visions International Entertainment Limited

The Author asserts the moral right to be identified as the author of this work

And after all that legal stuff, we hope you enjoy it.

Visions International Entertainment Ltd
The Billiard Room, Parklands Farm, Lower Green
Chelmsford, Essex CM2 8QS
e-mail: deltic15@aol.com

For details of other bus and transport-related products, please visit the Visions web site:
http://www.visionsinternational.biz

CONTENTS

INTRODUCTION

Fifty years ago, London Transport's green Country Area buses, and Green Line coaches, were hived off from the London Transport "empire". From 1st January 1970, they became part of the National Bus Company, forming its subsidiary London Country Bus Services Ltd.

Upon the formation of the London Passenger Transport Board in 1933, bus services beyond Greater London in the home counties, around London to a distance of some thirty to forty miles out from the centre, were taken over by the new entity. Not only did these include those operated by London General Country Services (which was allied to the major bus operator within Greater London, the London General Omnibus Company), but also routes which had been in the domain of such major operators as Eastern National, Maidstone & District, Aldershot & District and Thames Valley. These were formed into the Country Area of the L.P.T.B. which also took over the recently-formed Green Line coach network, comprising limited-stop services which radiated from central London, or crossed Greater London. In contrast to the familiar red-liveried buses serving Greater London itself, a livery of Lincoln green was adopted for the Country buses, initially with white relief as opposed to cream on the red buses; with Green Line coaches similarly adorned, but with light green relief.

The fleet name "London Transport" was given to both Central Area red buses, and Country Area green ones, and along with the "bullseye" symbol used on bus stops, shelters and bus garages, a corporate identity was soon established for the new operator. Additionally, a programme of new garage building, which was already under way when the Country Area was created, was continued with many smart new premises being constructed until World War Two prevented this continuing.

In addition, all of the bus and coach routes taken over by the Country Bus department of London Transport were organised into a logical numbering sequence. Bus routes north of the Thames were numbered in the 300-399 series, whilst those in the south were given numbers from 400 to 499, although for some reason a number of routes running out to High Wycombe in the north-west were also numbered in the 400 series! Green Line coach routes initially were lettered, but when these were reinstated in 1946 (having been withdrawn for the duration of the war) they were given a new sequence of numbers, starting at 700. Finally, with the growth of new towns such as Harlow, Stevenage and Crawley in the 1950s, a new numbering series in the 800s was created for local services specifically serving them, starting at 800 for those in the northern part of the Country Area, and 850 for those in the southern.

After the war, once things had returned to normal, the fleet of Country Area buses and Green Line coaches - in common with the Central Area - reached the peak of standardisation. By 1955, with the exception of a few post-war 15T13 single-deckers, 76 lowbridge RLH class double-deckers needed for busy routes that passed beneath low railway bridges and 84 small GS-class single-deckers used for routes that were either sparsely trafficked or had restrictive clearances larger buses could not negotiate, all Country Area buses and coaches were of the RT and RF classes. With the addition of 69 RMC and 43 RCL class Routemaster coaches delivered in 1962/63 and 1965 for busy Green Line routes, and 100 RMLs which replaced RTs on busy Country Area bus routes, RTs and RFs still comprised the bulk of the fleet when it was taken over by the N.B.C. fifty years ago. The only more modern vehicles were eight XF-class Daimler Fleetline double-deckers, three similar XA-class Leyland Atlanteans and fourteen RC-class A.E.C. Reliances delivered in 1965 for experimental use, together with just over a hundred of the ill-fated MB and MBS class.

Batches of the similar, but smaller, SM class followed after the inception of London Country, having already been ordered by London Transport, and these made inroads into the RT fleet - nearly 500 of which had been inherited by the new operator. Also carrying on in the London Transport tradition, a batch of ninety Park Royal-bodied A.E.C. Reliances was delivered during the winter of 1971/72 comprising the RP class, which replaced the RCLs and RMCs on Green Line services - the latter being demoted to bus status and in turn replacing RTs.

It was in 1972 that the "new order" really kicked in for London Country, with the arrival of the small AF class of Daimler Fleetlines, and then the AN class Leyland Atlanteans. The first examples followed L.T. tradition by having three-piece front blind displays, though later batches of AN's had simpler displays, with three-track number blinds. As the 1970s progressed, London Country had batches of Bristol LH single-deckers, which became the BL and BN classes, as well as hundreds of Leyland National single-deckers. By accident or design, the last standard London Transport types (RMC and RML class Routemasters) were withdrawn by London Country early in 1980, though a solitary RF and a couple of XFs lingered on a few months longer.

The collection of photographs in this book from my archives show London Transport Country Area buses and Green Line coaches in the latter half of the 1960s, and then those that passed to London Country, or were delivered new to that operator, in the 1970s and early 1980s. They show them in their everyday working environment, and also illustrate how the once-standardised London Transport-origin fleet changed beyond recognition into just another National Bus Company subsidiary in just one decade. The pictures capture perfectly the atmosphere of London's Country buses and Green Line coaches forty to fifty or so years ago, and include a wealth of fascinating and unusual scenes, many having never been published before.

My thanks go to the P.S.V. Circle and the London Omnibus Traction Society, whose publications helped me keep track of the vehicles involved in the years the photographs were taken, as well as to the Ian's Bus Stop website for providing details of the newer vehicles which did not interest me then. As usual, may I also thank Colin Clarke who scanned my vast collection of negatives and slides to make this volume possible, as well as my publisher Ken Carr and Micheal J. McClelland for laying out the book. I would like to dedicate this volume to my new grand-daughter Ava McClellan, whose first birthday falls close to the anniversary of London Transport's loss of its Country Area and Green Line services.

Jim Blake
Palmers Green
4th October 2019

Main Cover Photo: A scene that could typify London Transport's Country Area buses between 1954 and 1969: RF617, GS42 and RT4782 (DS) stand in the small bus station outside their home garage, Dorking, on 5th June 1968. Only the modernised Green Line RF visible behind the RT gives away the fact that the picture was actually taken in the late 1960s! By coincidence, both RF617 and RT4782 became red Central Area buses in 1969, whilst the GS would be the last of its type in service in 1972.

Bottom Left Cover Photo: Still in smart condition and bearing the revised livery given London Country RTs in the early 1970s, RT3607 (ST) heads along South Street, Staines on 14th July 1976 on local route 441C. It is subbing for an RML, many of which were kaput at this time owing to a serious shortage of spare parts.

Bottom Right Cover Photo: On 23rd August 1978, RMC1517 (CM) heads through Hamsey Green on its way to Warlingham Park Hospital. By this time, busy route 403 was one of the last London Country major routes to be Routemaster operated. Skirting the edge of the old London Transport Central Area, it survives today as a London Buses route.

AT HOME

Country buses and Green Line coaches were housed in a number of garages , most of which were situated in major towns around their operating area. Typical was St. Albans Garage, one of the splendid new ones built in the 1930s. On 5th March 1966, GS54 (SA) is illuminated by spring sunshine when laying over there on local route 382, which served rural villages between St. Albans and Codicote. St. Albans Garage was sadly demolished in the 1990s despite efforts to preserve it as a working bus museum.

Route 321 linked St. Albans and Garston garage, outside the latter of which RT3011 (GR) stands in the evening sunshine on the same day. One of the GSs based there for such routes as the 309, 309A and 336A may just be discerned behind it. This splendid new garage was opened in 1952 to replace older garages in Watford High Street and Leavesden Road, and lasted until as recently as January 2019.

Hertford Garage was another of those built new in the 1930s, and on 30th March 1968, RT3692 (HG) stands outside it. Behind are two dead RTWs. These are probably having work done on them prior to export to Ceylon, this was often farmed out to Country Area garages in order to provide their fitters with overtime.

Leatherhead was one of the older Country Area garages, though had been equipped with new offices in the 1930s. On 31st March 1968, RF637 (LH) sets off from it for local route 419, shortly before further modernisation work to the premises began.

When built in 1939, the new Central Area garage at Gillingham Street, Victoria was provided with a basement area intended to house Green Line coaches, many of which served the nearby Eccleston Bridge coach station. Owing to the outbreak of war, it never happened after all. However, in later years a Green Line RF was based at the garage to act as a standby to cover any breakdowns. On 8th April 1968, modernised RF143 (GM) accompanies two London Transport service vans in the garage yard. It had a restricted blind display in order to accommodate a blind showing most Green Line routes and destinations which it might have to serve. Riverside Garage at Hammersmith also housed a Green Line coach for emergency use.

Swanley Garage was little more than a large shed, with adjacent modern offices. On 2nd May 1968, RT3002 (SJ) is one of three parked up inside it. This was one of a number of formerly red RTs overhauled in 1963/64 with early RT3/1 bodies in green livery, to replace older roofbox RT3/3 and RT10-bodied vehicles. By now, they were due for withdrawal, although in the event some lasted well into London Country days. In this view, the fire extinguishers and watering can, just inside the door of the garage, are of note.

Dorking Garage was another of the splendid new ones built in the 1930s. It incorporated offices and waiting rooms, the latter being useful for people waiting for the Green Line coaches that terminated there and ventured to such faraway places as Luton and Dunstable. On 9th May 1968, little GS42 (DS) however is only going to the nearby village of Ranmore on local route 433.

On the same day as the previous picture, RT3700 and RT3309 (LH) are nearest the camera in a group of RTs parked in the rain in the rear yard of Leatherhead Garage. This garage operated three important trunk routes at the time, the 406, 408 and 470. Of note is the large slipboard on RT3700 - it shows that route 418, a Country route that ventured into the Central Area, had protected fares on that section of route. This meant that short-distance fares were not charged, in order to reserve the buses, in effect, for longer distance passengers.

One of the most impressive of the Country Area's garages was Windsor, and it too had a small bus and coach station attached, with waiting facilities for Green Line passengers. On 1st June 1968, RT4440 (WR) faces out of the rear exit of the garage, and is probably a spreadover bus on route 457A, usually at this time operated by RMLs like the one accompanying it which had entered service there in the spring of 1966.

On 14th February 1969, RT4270 (HH) has also been working a spreadover duty and stands beside the offices at Two Waters (Hemel Hempstead) Garage. Their architecture was typical of the 1930's Country Area garages, of which this was yet another. The day after this picture was taken, new O.M.O. MBSs replaced RTs on such routes as the 314 and 314A.

Exemplifying how vehicle type allocations to routes were not as rigid in the Country Area as in the Central Area, RF271 and RT4744 (DS) have both been operating route 414 when standing in the rear yard of Dorking Garage on 26th October 1969. This was a long trunk route, running all the way from West Croydon to Horsham via Dorking. By this time, whilst RTs still operated it during the week, O.M.O. RFs were used on Sundays. This particular RF was one of many former Green Line coaches downgraded to bus status in the mid-1960s, though retaining their coach seats.

Addlestone Garage was yet another of the new Country Area garages built in the 1930s. On the evening of 28th July 1970, RLH24 (WY) is one of three of its class which have run in after the rush hour. They will never run in service again, since next day they were replaced by new SMs. RF666 (WY) will however see two more years' service.

The modern Stevenage Garage was opened in 1959 to serve the ever-expanding New Town. Winter sunlight illuminates RF577 and RF597 (SV) inside it on 29th December 1972. Behind them are a group of yellow and blue-liveried SMs used on the New Town "Superbus" services.

Illustrating the design of the shed of Stevenage Garage, which was very similar to that at Hatfield opened in the same year, and also the newer part of Grays Garage, RT626 (SV) stands outside on 29th May 1974. This was one of a handful of RTs retained there after most of them had been replaced by ANs on New Town services in October 1972, needed to operate works services under a bridge carrying the Great Northern main line over the old Great North Road at Little Wymondley, which was too low to accommodate the ANs. This view also shows the garage offices flanking the main road; a Leyland National stands between them and the garage shed.

With a Green Line RP and a Superbus SM behind it, RF294 (HG) sets off from Stevenage Garage on route 386, which traversed country lanes and served rural villages in the area rather than travelling direct to Hitchin via the Great North Road. The large building in the distance is part of the Stevenage Industrial Area, the other side of the track of the Great Northern main line from the New Town. By now, a new railway station had been opened at this location, more convenient for the New Town than the original which was at the northern end of the Old Town, itself north of the New Town.

Nicely illustrating a variety of vehicle types parked outside Garston Garage on 13th September 1978, RML2450 (GR) is flanked by MB104 and AN9. The side advert on the RML is for a day rover ticket valid on all National Bus Company fleets - I wonder how far it was possible to get from the London Country area on them?

Also towards the end of London Country Routemaster operation, RMC1511 and RCL2251 (GY) stand inside Grays Garage on 15th September 1978. Both types had once operated from there on Green Line routes, but now were being used as spare cover for O.P.O. types. The RCL is one of a number still in Lincoln green livery.

How the mighty have fallen! New less than eight years previously to replace coach Routemasters on Green Line services, RP85 (DG) stands in the yard of Dunton Green Garage on 1st March 1980, having apparently worked local route 471 which was once the preserve of GSs. Another of the type stands at the back of the yard out of action. The ninety RPs were not a success, and their demotion to bus duties, and early demise, was hastened by the introduction of new, "luxury coach" Reliances of the RB and RS classes towards the end of the 1970s.

CHURCHES

Country Area buses served many towns which had impressive churches. A good example is this one in Gravesend town centre, where RT3447 (NF) calls on local route 495 on 6th April 1968.

St. Peters Street is the main shopping street in St. Albans, and takes its name from the parish church. This forms a backdrop to this view of RF303 (SA) terminating there on route 304 on 14th February 1969. This RF had originally been Country bus RF522, but was renumbered when converted to a Green Line coach in 1956. Bizarrely, when it and the others in its batch were converted back to Country buses in the mid-1960s, they were not renumbered!

On 3rd May 1969, a well-filled RF203 (WR) has a long way to go to reach Windsor on Green Line route 718. Modernised in 1967, it has recently been downgraded to bus status and adorned with a yellow waistband and "London Transport" fleet names. It passes the impressive St. John The Baptist parish church at the southern end of Epping High Street.

One of the southern extremities of the Country Area was Wrotham in Kent, where Green Line route 717 terminated. When this was withdrawn in late 1968, the 719 was extended to replace it, giving a long cross-London route to and from Hemel Hempstead. On 3rd April 1972, bus RF584 (SJ) has been pressed into service on this route and stands at its terminus beside St. John's Parish Church, Wrotham.

RT1012 (CM), another one of the three that would gain N.B.C. corporate livery in 1977, turns from Bartlett Street into Brighton Road, South Croydon, when heading for West Croydon on a short journey of route 403 on 18th August 1973. The large building on the left is South Croydon Methodist Church.

RF281 (NF) was the highest-numbered Green Line RF to be modernised. On 18th July 1974, it hurries past Dartford's parish church, the Church of the Holy Trinity, on its long journey to Gravesend. This RF is smartly preserved today.

A well-known landmark on London Road, Bushey Heath is St. Peter's Church at the junction with Elstree Road. RML2424 (GR) passes it working route 306 on 10th July 1975. Sadly, this was one of two complete RMLs which London Country sold for scrap four years later, perhaps to force London Transport's hand in buying the rest - merely for Schadenfreude?

Early London Country Leyland Atlantean AN117 (GY) collects passengers at the Rainham terminus of route 328, outside the historic parish church of St. Helen and St. Giles, on 1st April 1976. Its livery is green and yellow, as adopted when these vehicles were first introduced in 1972.

REINCARNATION

During 1966/67, a remarkable "reincarnation" of the majority of the surviving Green Line RFs took place. Following the appearance of the fourteen experimental RC-class A.E.C. Reliance Green Line coaches, London Transport were not happy with them, so instead of ordering more to replace the RF coach fleet - then some fourteen or fifteen years old - refurbished the RFs instead and incorporated some of the features embodied in the newer vehicles. These included fluorescent saloon lighting, twin headlamps and a broad waistband which was painted light green and carried a new-style Green Line fleet name. Work was done at Aldenham, involving a light overhaul without body change. Their change in appearance was such that many people thought they were new! RF176 (RG) illustrates this perfectly when passing County Hall's Addington Street Annexe at Waterloo on its long journey from High Wycombe to Reigate on route 711 on 16th September 1967.

Similarly refurbished and still looking smart some months later, RF245 (ST) attracts the attention of an inspector when calling at Hammersmith Butterwick bus and Green Line coach station on its way to Sunningdale on a gloomy 27th December 1967 - my 20th birthday.

As mentioned earlier, some modernised Green Line coaches were demoted to bus status only a year or so after being done. They retained their canary yellow waistbands when they passed to London Country, with the new fleet name replacing the London Transport one, and the LT bullseyes on the front were painted out. One of these, RF26 (DS) - numerically the first Green Line RF to be built, passes through Purley Cross on Easter Sunday 5th April 1970, on the Sunday O.M.O. working of the long route 414 from West Croydon to Horsham. This RF survived into preservation.

Subsequently, modernised RFs gained the L.C.B.S. "flying Polo" symbol where the LT "bullseye" had been. RF165 (SV) illustrates this on 18th March 1973 when working one of the Sunday trips on route 303 from Stevenage, whose bus station it is leaving, to Hitchin. It is still in Green Line livery, and though by now most such RFs were officially downgraded to bus status irrespective of livery, they were frequently called upon to cover for defective RPs and Leyland Nationals on Green Line routes.

PUBS

Pubs featured on many Country Area bus and Green Line coach routes, either as timing points of termini. A good example of the former was The Cherry Tree at Welwyn Garden City, just before the railway bridge taking buses across the Great Northern main line. On 27th April 1968, RT2850 (HF) collects passengers there on local route 340A. It is one of the formerly red RT3/1-bodied RTs transferred to the Country Area in 1963/64. This one was appropriated as an staff bus in 1969, still running in green livery. Regrettably, this splendid 1930's pub was demolished and replaced by a Waitrose superstore in 1990.

The Duke's Head in Addlestone, at the crossroads of Station Road and Brighton Road just west of the garage, was also a timing point and where buses whose routes did not actually pass the garage changed crew. On 9th May 1968, RLH14 (GF) passes it on its way from Guildford to Staines on route 436. By now, this was one of only two of the 1950 batch of RLH's still in service. This pub too is no more, replaced by flats in 1995.

Gravesend, like many traditional English towns, had several pubs in its town centre. On 5th March 1969, RT4121 (NF) turns from New Road into Darnley Road between The Sun, a Truman's house, and The Wheatsheaf, a Charrington's. Sadly, the Sun closed in 1970 and was subsequently demolished, but happily The Wheatsheaf is still going strong. As regards RT4121, it was overhauled as a red bus after being displaced by new MBSs on Gravesend local services shortly after this picture was taken.

Dating back to the 17th century, the Spread Eagle Inn and hotel in the centre of Epsom is probably doing a roaring trade on Derby Day, 5th June 1974, as a packed RT4344 (GD) brings spectators back from the races to Epsom Station on a short working of the 406, rather than the race special 406F. It has been loaned to Godstone Garage for the day. Sadly, this pub too has since perished, closing in the early 1990s and the site used for retail purposes today.

Standing in for a defunct RML on route 452 (a renumbering of the 457A) RT2722 (WR) passes the General Eliot pub just outside Uxbridge town centre on its way to Windsor on 16th July 1975. This pleasant pub, alongside the Grand Union Canal, is still with us today.

On 20th September 1975, RCL2226 (GD) - one of three kept at Godstone Garage for route 709 - works an extra on the 705 bring spectators home from the Biggin Hill Air Display. It is passing the Mark Inn at Keston, which closed in 2008. The building is now in residential use.

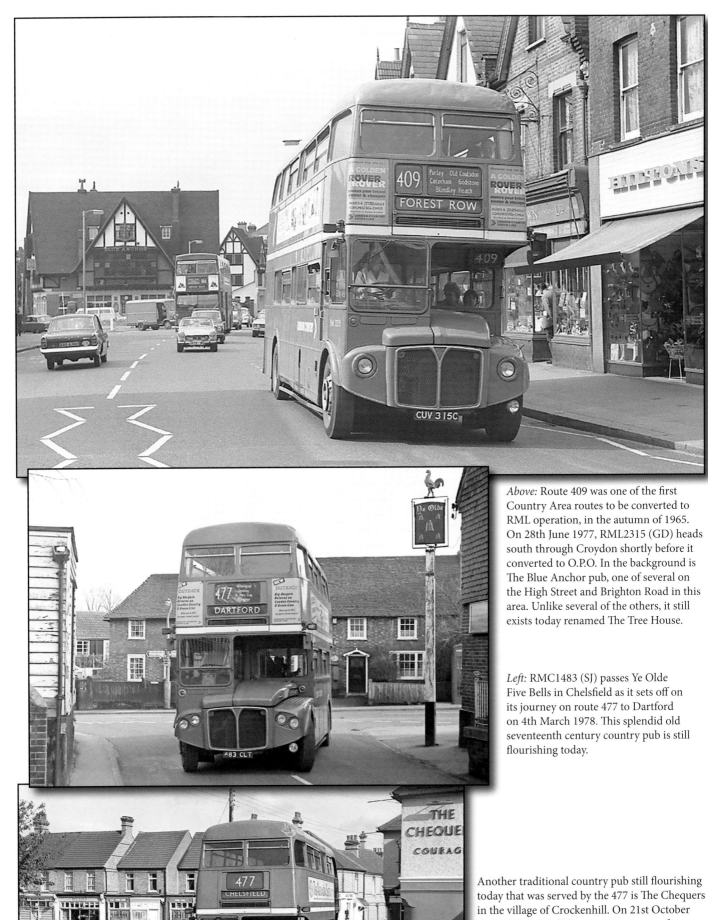

Above: Route 409 was one of the first Country Area routes to be converted to RML operation, in the autumn of 1965. On 28th June 1977, RML2315 (GD) heads south through Croydon shortly before it converted to O.P.O. In the background is The Blue Anchor pub, one of several on the High Street and Brighton Road in this area. Unlike several of the others, it still exists today renamed The Tree House.

Left: RMC1483 (SJ) passes Ye Olde Five Bells in Chelsfield as it sets off on its journey on route 477 to Dartford on 4th March 1978. This splendid old seventeenth century country pub is still flourishing today.

Another traditional country pub still flourishing today that was served by the 477 is The Chequers in the village of Crockenhill. On 21st October 1979, RMC1492 (SJ) passes it on its way from Dartford to Chelsfield.

OLD TOWN

London Transport's Country Area, and thus its successor London Country, served many historic and important towns in the Home Counties. Typical of them was St. Albans, along whose St. Peters Street RF110 (RE) heads on the northern peripheral Green Line route 724 on its long journey from High Wycombe to Romford on 20th January 1968.

Hertford, the county town of Hertfordshire, was also another important centre of Country Area operation. On 5th April 1968, GS65 (HG) collects passengers in its High Street on route 388, which served rural villages between there and Welwyn Garden City.

The historic Surrey town of Reigate would house the headquarters of London Country Bus Services in later years, just as it had been the home of London General Country Services and, before that, East Surrey. Still in the London Transport era, RT4741 (RG) heads along its High Street on local route 430 on 9th May 1968.

Left: The Surrey town of Leatherhead also featured prominently in Country bus operation. On 5th June 1968, RT3311 (LH) heads through the town centre running in to its garage off route 406.

Below: The Berkshire town of Slough was served by both London Transport/London Country and Thames Valley buses - the latter heading for towns to its west such as Maidenhead and Reading. Most of the local services were operated by the former, including route 400. With an unusual via blind display, RT3118 (WR) stands in for an RML in the town centre on 8th March 1969, shortly before this route converted to MBS O.M.O.

Dorking in Surry was a centre of Country bus operation, too. With the North Downs visible in the background, former Green Line RF236 (DS) heads along Dorking High Street on local route 449 on 25th May 1970.

Surrey's county town, Guildford, was served by both London Transport/London Country and Aldershot & District - the latter operating services to the south and west of it. Also on 27th May 1970, RF595 (GF) passes through the town centre on route 432, which linked Guildford with Great Bookham.

The Hertfordshire market town of Hitchin was one of the northernmost extremities of the London Transport and London Country systems. On 13th July 1972, RT981 (SV) heads out of the town on route 801A, one of the complicated Stevenage New Town services that linked both Hitchin and the New Town with the Industrial Area.

The old town of Stevenage was situated on the Great North Road to the north of the New Town. On 12th October 1972, RT2208 (SV) heads through it on the New Town circular route 800, bound for the old Stevenage railway station, which was at the northern end of the old town. It was replaced in the summer of 1973 by a new one adjacent to the New Town centre.

The old town of Hemel Hempstead was also situated to the north of its new town. On 4th October 1972, RT1044 (HH) heads though its High Street on local route 312.

NEW TOWN

A number of new towns were established in the area served by London Transport's Country buses in the early post-war years, to accommodate London's "overspill" population. One was at Hemel Hempstead in Hertfordshire, through whose main shopping street, Marlowes, RT940 (HH) sets off for Watford Heath on a very wet 30th March 1968.

Harlow in Essex was one of the largest New Towns. In its bus station on 6th April 1968, RT635 (HA) loads up on town service 804, in the new series of route numbers set up for such services. It is one of the RTs painted in Green Line livery to act as rush hour "reliefs" on busy routes, but in this case is subbing for an RML.

Stevenage, another Hertfordshire town, was the first New Town established after the war - much to the consternation of its indigenous residents. Although its town centre and bus station, where RT3425 (SV) collects passengers on town service 800 on 27th April 1968, were adjacent to the Great Northern main line, no railway station serving it was built until 1973, residents having to use the existing one, a couple of miles to the north at the far end of the old town. This was a common problem with new towns. As regards this RT, it has one of the white fleetnames various buses were given on overhaul or repaint in the summer of 1966, and its blind display is scanty to say the least!

Left: The principal new town served by the southern area of the Country bus network was Crawley in Sussex, on the border between the London Transport and Southdown Motor Services' operating areas. On 27th May 1970, RT3693 (CY) passes through its industrial area, again with a somewhat uninformative blind display!

Centre: A well-loaded RT4401 (CY) calls at Crawley Bus Station also on 27th May 1970 on local route 426A. This was one of the formerly red RTs overhauled as Country buses with RT3/1 bodies (the earliest type without roofboxes) to replace roofbox vehicles in 1963/64. Although earmarked for withdrawal in 1968, it not only remained in service with London Country until 1972, but was one of three RT3/1s sold back to London Transport in September that year and remained in use until the spring of 1978, when its body was almost thirty years old.

Below: By 1972, Stevenage New Town's services had become very confusing and complicated indeed. Route 800, which had replaced the 392A (a route I knew well since I had relatives who had been resettled on its route in 1956) in 1964, not only operated a loop in conjunction with route 801 around Bedwell and Bandley Hill, but also served a newer part of the New Town, Martin's Wood. On 13th July 1972, RT4105 (SV) loads up with shoppers in Archer Road on that part of the 800. Three months later, most of the RTs working at Stevenage New Town were replaced by O.M.O. ANs and the services were simplified.

In far better weather conditions that illustrated in the earlier picture of this route, RT4107 (HH) heads along Marlowes, Hemel Hempstead New Town's main shopping street on the 302 on 5th October 1972. RTs would work this, and sister route 301, for a few more years yet.

Harlow New Town still had predominantly older ex-London Transport buses serving it in 1974. Adorned in ill-suited N.B.C. corporate livery, RF310 (HA) heads along Fourth Avenue in the New Town centre on 7th June that year, working local route 380.

Roundabouts were a feature of the new towns in an effort to ease traffic flow. Also on 7th June 1974, RT621 (HA) tackles that at the junction of Fourth Avenue, First Avenue and Fifth Avenue on a short working of trunk route 339 to Ongar, Two Brewers.

Very late in the day, a number of new New Town services were introduced to serve new parts of Harlow New Town. One was the 807, on which RT1700 (HA) approaches Harlow Bus Station also on 7th June 1974. This RT is still active in the area today, one of the London Bus Company's heritage fleet which services the Epping Ongar Railway.

Long after most RTs had been replaced by newer vehicles at Stevenage, a handful of them as well as RFs remained based there. Of the latter, modernised ex-Green Line RF102 (SV) awaits departure from the bus station on route 384, which meandered all the way from Hertford to Letchworth via various country villages. It contrasts with more modern vehicles, for which RFs often had to stand in, on the Superbus services in the background. Letchworth was one of the northernmost towns of all on the Country Area/ London Country network.

SCHOOL BUS

London's Country buses, of course, carried lots of children to and from school and in fact operated a number of special school routes. However on 14th May 1968, GS33 (GR) loads up with schoolchildren in Rickmansworth High Street on "normal" route 309. This did not need the small GS class, and was also worked by RFs, and whether it had room for all the smartly-uniformed straw-hatted schoolgirls attempting to board we shall never know!

A fortnight later, on 28th May 1968, Green Line-liveried RT1021 (NF) sets off from Gravesend Clocktower on special school route 497, to collect homegoing pupils from Dover Road schools in Northfleet.

Left: Illustrating how such special school routes interworked with ordinary Country bus services, RT1021 (NF) has returned to Gravesend, and loads up with passengers on route 498, running to Northfleet, Plough via Painters Ash Estate.

Below: A number of schools on the outskirts of Watford had dedicated routes, as well as journeys diverted off ordinary services. On 20th June 1974, RMC1495 (HH) has actually terminated within the confines of Queens School working a journey from there on trunk route 301 to Hemel Hempstead, with unfortunately badly set blinds.

Route 346C was one of a number of dedicated school routes in the Watford area, and was limited stop. On 30th April 1975, RML2423 (WR) heads along Aldenham Road, Bushey to pick up pupils. The 346 group of routes had converted from RT to RML in the spring of 1966, but by this time many were defunct and other types had to be used. Unfortunately, this RML was one of two which, though mechanically complete, were sold for scrap by London Country in the summer of 1979.

Above: Back at Queens School, AN53 (GR) is about to turn into its forecourt on a school journey of local route 385. This had converted from RT to AN operation in the summer of 1972.

Right: At almost the same spot as the previous picture, RMC1487 (HH) works a school journey on route 302, bound for Hemel Hempstead. I was a co-owner of this RMC in the mid-1980s when it resided at the ill-fated Docklands Road Transport Museum.

Also on 6th November 1975, RT2779 (GR) loads up outside Queens School on a school journey of route 311. Supposedly RML-operated, this route was entirely RT-worked on this occasion, since so many of the RMLs at Garston Garage (to where it is heading) were out of action due to the mid-1970s spares shortage!

Some of the last coach Routemasters based at Grays Garage were used on "school special" duties. On 15th September 1978, RCL2249 (GY) sets off from Grays Garage on one of these trips, having recently been transferred there from Chelsham.

A week later, on 22nd September 1978, RMC1483 (SJ) on its way from Chelsfield to Dartford passes RMC1493 (SJ) in Crockenhill village. The latter has terminated there on a school journey - this involved a three-point turn and reversal and is one of the reasons why route 477 retained RMCs until almost the end of crew operation with London Country.

INDUSTRIAL AREAS

Country buses also operated a number of special routes serving factories and industrial estates. One of the best-known was that established at Stevenage New Town, on the other side of the track of the Great Northern main line from the town centre. A very confusing network of routes served it, linking it with not just the New Town but also Stevenage old town and Hitchin. RT981 (SV) loads up in Gunnels Wood Road to take homegoing workers to the latter town on 13th July 1972 on route 800A. Of note are the words "Industrial Area" beneath its number blind, making it clear that this route served it.

Also in Gunnels Wood Road, but on 5th October 1972, RT4105 (SV) works Industrial Area route 802B bound for Sishes End, overtaking "Superbus" SM460 (SV) on route SB2. Ten days later, most of Stevenage's RTs were replaced by new O.M.O. ANs, as mentioned earlier.

Left: RT981 (SV) was one of three RTs retained at Stevenage, which were needed to work journeys on routes 303 and 303C from the Industrial Area to Hitchin, passing beneath the low railway bridge at Little Wymondley, for which ANs were too tall. It collects passengers at a very wet Gunnels Wood Road on 2nd May 1975. This situation was resolved the following year when Leyland National single-deckers took these journeys over.

Below: A number of routes in the Grays and Tilbury areas also served industrial facilities. On 1st April 1976, RCL2241 (GY) is actually working special rush hour route 329 at the purpose-built bus station serving the huge Thames Board Mills at East Purfleet, visible behind it and RMC1471 (GY), but evidently does not have a blind display for this recently-introduced route, so shows 328 instead.

Lots of industrial premises existed on the opposite bank of the Thames, too, notably paper mills at Greenhithe and Horns Cross. At the latter point, a somewhat faded N.B.C.-liveried RML2349 (NF) does a three-point turn to collect homegoing workers bound for Dartford and Crayford where, unusually, it is also turning short. The date is 22nd September 1978.

HOSPITAL SERVICES

As well as for schools and industrial premises, Country buses also operated a number of special services for hospitals. Many of these had been established in late Victorian times on the outskirts of London, particularly "lunatic asylums" and "fever hospitals" - latterly more kindly referred to as "mental hospitals" and "isolation hospitals". All is quiet in St. Peters Street, St. Albans on Sunday 18th August 1968, as RT1103 (SA) heads for Harperbury Hospital - a mental hospital built on a former World War One airfield near Shenley in the 1920s. Today, much of its area has been replaced by new housing.

For many years, special limited stop hospital route 808 linked Stevenage New Town with a number of hospitals in the Hitchin area. On 24th May 1970, RT1023 (SV) heads along Valley Way, Leaves Spring on its way back to Chells.

On the other side of London, a large complex of buildings housing mental patients existed at Bexley Hospital. This was served by Sunday-only Central Area bus route 124A, and journeys diverted off Country Area trunk route 401, which ran all the way from Upper Belvedere to Sevenoaks. On 31st May 1971, RT3734 (SJ) stands at the hospital gates on one of the latter. Are the people standing around patients or visitors - or bus enthusiasts?! Most of this hospital's area, too, has been given over to housing in recent years.

Napsbury Hopsital was another in the Watford area catering for the mentally ill, located near London Colney having been originally known as the Middlesex County Asylum. It too had a special limited stop bus service, the 345. On 29th May 1974, RT4102 (GR) passes beneath the famous Bushey Arches on its way there. This hospital too has since closed, its site taken over by residential development.

Netherne Hospital near Coulsdon was yet another mental hospital that merited its own limited stop bus service. On 5th June 1974, N.B.C.-liveried RF621 (LH) heads through Epsom Town Centre on its way there. This hospital closed in 1994 and once again residential development replaced it, known as Netherne-On-The-Hill.

On a murky 28th February 1976, Maidstone Corporation Massey-bodied Leyland Titan PD2 No.14 is one of several on loan to London Country, covering for defunct RMCs at Dartford Garage on route 499. It arrives at Joyce Green Hospital, originally an isolation hospital near the banks of the Thames. It was closed in 2000 and subsequently demolished.

One of the best-known hospital termini served by Country Area buses was Warlingham Park Hospital, at which RT1027 (CM) arrives on 1st May 1976 on the 403. It was the eastern terminus of trunk routes 408 and 472 for many years, too. Opened as Croydon Mental Hospital in 1903, it closed in 1999 and today the plush Greatpark housing development covers the site.

Joyce Green Hospital was also served by journeys on route 477. On a very bleak 9th December 1979, RMC1512 (SJ) arrives there. Just under three months later, this would be the last RMC to operate for London Country.

TERMINUS

Termini of Country bus and Green Line coach routes varied greatly, from main roads in major towns to bus stations in new towns, or from obscure country villages to the garages from which they operated. In the latter case, RT609 (SA) stands in the small bus station in front of its home garage, St. Albans, on 5th March 1966. Route 313 still exists today, but as a red London Buses route running from Potters Bar to Chingford via Enfield.

Various attempts were made to provide Country bus and Green Line coach services through the Dartford Tunnel, which opened in 1963. Initially RTs were used on new route 300, but patronage was so low that GSs replaced them on route 399. GS21 (GY) stands at its Grays War Memorial terminus on 10th September 1966. This was little used too, and eventually London Transport gave up the ghost.

Route 406F was for many years a special service connecting Epsom Station with Epsom racecourse, but journeys on route 406 also terminated at Epsom Downs on Derby Day from the other direction. On 7th June 1967, RT4548 (RG) stands at the special terminus for buses bound for Redhill. The unusual pole-mounted bus stop flag is of note. This RT was subsequently overhauled as a red bus.

A small bus station, with waiting facilities, existed adjacent to Welwyn Garden City Station on the Great Northern main line. On 27th April 1968, GS13 (HG) has terminated there on route 388, which meandered its way across the Hertfordshire countryside from Hertford, serving such picturesque villages as Tewin. This GS is one of many preserved today - and who was it that once said that out of the 84 GSs built, no fewer than 97 were preserved?!

A number of Country Area bus routes terminated at Rickmansworth Station, served in 1968 by Metropolitan Line A-Stock Underground trains to and from Amersham, and B.R. DMUs between Marylebone and Aylesbury. On 14th May 1968, RF687 (GR) stands there amid works to revise the road layout adjacent to the station.

In Gravesend, a number of Country bus and Green Line coach routes terminated at the Clock Tower, generally arriving from the west and south - with Maidstone & District buses continuing eastwards - this was a "border town" in which that operator also had a garage. On 28th May 1968, GS28 (NF) and RF594 (NF) stand in an adjacent side street used as a terminus on Country routes 451 and 489A respectively.

Above: In Slough, a side street off the main Windsor Road served as a terminus for short-working buses on route 441. On 1st June 1968, RT3011 (WR), another formerly red RT3/1 overhauled in green in 1963/64, stands there on a short working to Hedgerley Village.

Left: RT740 (HH) is yet another formerly red RT3/1, and stands at the Queen Elizabeth Hospital terminus in Welwyn Garden City used by local routes 324 and 340A, and trunk routes 330 and 330A, on 21st July 1968. The latter routes ran to St. Albans and Hemel Hempstead.

Both Central Area and Country Area buses terminated at Orpington Station, using a small turning circle on its down (southbound) side. On 20th September 1969, RF117 (DG), one of several Green Line coaches downgraded to bus status in the mid-1960s, loads up on route 431 bound for Sevenoaks.

Romford (London Road) Garage was unusual in that, firstly, a large Victorian house, visible on the right here, had been appropriated as its offices and staff facilities and, secondly, that it only operated Green Line coaches. It was also the only Country Area/London Country garage situated within a London Borough. However, its forecourt was used as the terminus for busy trunk route 370, on which RT1000 (GY) and RT3675 (GY) stand on 28th December 1971. Eastern National routes serving Romford also terminated there.

Typical of fringe developments around country towns was the Millway Estate near Garston. It was served by local route 385, on which RT4113 (GR) stands at its terminus on 13th July 1972. Next day, this RT was withdrawn when the 321 and 385 group of routes converted to AN O.M.O. However it was one of 34 sold back to London Transport to cover shortages two months later.

On the same day, RT3631 (LS) accompanies an RF on route 364 and another RT on route 360 at the Luton, Park Square terminus used for Country buses and Green Line coaches in the Bedfordshire town. Both their own Luton Garage and United Counties' premises were nearby. The 321 usually worked in two overlapping sections, the southern portion running between Uxbridge and St. Albans. As so often happened, this RT has an inappropriate via blind for the long run to Maple Cross!

In its later years, Green Line coach route 709 terminated from the south at Baker Street Station, and ran only during Monday to Friday rush hours and on Sundays. On 30th May 1973, RCL2237 (GD) stands at the Allsop Place terminus, outside the London Transport canteen, which served bus and Underground staff alike and was also a training centre for LT's in-house catering staff.

Other post-war housing development around Watford took place at Leavesden, where RT2157 (GR) stands at the Ganders Ash terminus of route 306 on 6th November 1975. As with route 311 illustrated earlier, this route had converted to RML operation in the spring of 1966, but so many of these vehicles were off the road owing the extreme shortage of vehicle spares at this period, that it effectively reverted to RT operation.

Aveley was another post-war housing development served by the Country Area and its successor London Country. On a rather bleak 28th February 1976, downgraded modernised RF88 (GY) stands at Aveley, Usk Road terminus working local route 371A to Tilbury, Feenan Highway. As with the RTs at Garston, RFs were having to cover for much newer vehicles throughout the London Country system in the mid-1970s. The typical London Transport Country Area timber bus shelter, and the bullseye sign still on it more than six years after the LT/LCBS split, are also of note.

At a time when many RMLs at Northfleet Garage were becoming very scruffy, RML2322 (NF) appears to have been recently repainted in N.B.C. corporate green livery when standing at the 480's Erith terminus. It is somewhat odd that the standard LT "bullseye" bus stop flag has been replaced by an NBC one, still using the LT post, even though this terminus is well within Greater London!

As mentioned earlier, Country route 403 skirted the edge of the Central Area and still exists today as a London Buses (red) route. Its western terminus was in Belmont Road, Wallington, where RCL2238 (CM) has arrived on 24th April 1978. This was shared with such Central Area routes as the 115 and the southern section of the 77 and 77B.

Above: Shortly before their replacement by the short-lived BT class Bristol VRs on route 370, RCL2248 (GY) shares the Romford London Road Garage stand with an Eastern National Bristol FLF Lodekka on 30th May 1977. The garage was closed not long afterwards.

Left: Although RF507 on route 218 at the end of March 1979 is widely believed to have been the last RF in normal service, this is true only of the London Transport fleet, since RF202 (NF) survived it by a couple of months working routes 489 and 490 from Northfleet Garage. On 24th May 1979, this downgraded modernised Green Line RF stands at The White Swan terminus in the village of Ash, prior to running in to its garage. It was subsequently restored to 1967 Green Line livery and used on London Country's ramblers bus services for a couple of years, and then as a special events vehicle prior to passing into preservation proper.

A number of outlying termini in the Country Area were provided with turning circles and lay-by's in which buses could stand. On 30th August 1979, RML2348 (WR) stands on one of these at local Slough route 407's Cippenham terminus. This was the westernmost point reached by London Transport and London Country buses in the Slough area, having originally been served by Thames Valley.

INTERCHANGE

Interchange between bus, coach and railway services has always been an important aspect of passenger transport in London. A good example of this is the two bus stations and Southern Region railway station in Kingston-Upon-Thames. On 25th November 1967, modernised Green Line RF175 (RG) passes the railway station, still nearly twenty years after nationalisation showing the name Southern RAILWAY, working the recently-introduced Airport Express route 727. One bus station was directly behind the railway station on the left, the other behind where I was standing to take this photograph. Today, Kingston still has two bus stations, one across the road from this point on the right backing on to the railway line, the other in a different part of the town.

At Welwyn Garden City, interchange with the Great Northern main line's local services was provided by stops on the bridge by The Cherry Tree pub, or for terminating buses at a small bus station adjacent to the railway station. On 27th April 1968, RT2326 (HH) crosses the bridge on the busy 330. Of note is its white fleet name, applied on repaint in the summer of 1966.

Buses passing through Addlestone called at the Southern Region station, but were sometimes delayed by trains having right of way at the level crossing. On 9th May 1968, RLH31 (WY) crosses it on route 461 on its way to Staines.

Above: Back at Welwyn Garden City, GS55 (HG) stands at the small bus station and is about to work a short journey on route 388 to the village of Tewin on 27th June 1968. This GS also survives in preservation. The stop flag tells us that Green Line route 716A and the limited stop 803 also terminated at it.

Left: Rickmansworth was an important interchange point between the Metropolitan Line and (originally) Great Central main line trains and various local bus services calling at the station. On 24th August 1969, RT3081 (LS) arrives there on the long 321 trunk route bound for Uxbridge. This RT had an odd livery with not only a white fleet name, but also a light green waistband instead of a cream one. This led many people to believe it had been a Green Line RT which, in fact, it never was - it had originally been red.

Above: Another Metropolitan Line station which provided interchange with various Country bus and Green Line coach routes was Croxley on the Watford branch. On 12th July 1972, RF614 (HH) calls there on route 318, and is terminating at the nearby Croxley Green Midland Region station. After many years planning and no doubt much expense, plans to link the two lines and run Metropolitan Line trains into Watford Junction appear to have been sabotaged in recent times.

Right: In the late 1960s and early 1970s, the bus station adjacent to Kingston Southern Region Station was used as a terminus for Central Area bus routes 14 (Sunday), 57, 85, 200, 213 and 213A, and Country routes 406, 406A and 418. On 22nd September 1972, RT4202 (LH) sets off for Redhill on the 406, leaving an SM on the 418 on the stand. Other bus routes and Green Line coaches passing through Kingston stopped outside.

Tadworth Station, on the Southern Region's Tattenham Corner branch, was the terminus of route 416, which ran to Epsom and Esher. On 23rd February 1973, RF576 (LH) loads up there, whilst RT2722 (LH) works one of many short journeys on the 406 which also terminated there.

Caterham-On-The-Hill is the terminus of another former Southern Railway commuter branch, and on 18th August 1973, RF542 (RG) calls there on local route 440 bound for Woldingham as RML2333 (GD) arrives on its way from West Croydon to Reigate on the 411. The latter has recently been overhauled in the new corporate NBC livery.

Watford Junction station is an important interchange between West Coast Main Line and local train services and local bus and Green Line routes. On 4th June 1974, when buses still used side streets nearby as their terminus, RF564 (HH) sets off for Hemel Hempstead on the scenic route 322. Work is about to begin on a major rebuild of the station, and construction of a purpose-built bus station adjacent to it, on the right behind the RF.

Some of the routes serving nearby industrial areas terminated at Ockendon Station, providing interchange with local services on the Tilbury lines. On 1st April 1976, RMC1470 (GY) sets off from there on weekday route 369, as one of the original LT&S slam-door EMUs stands in the station.

A number of bus routes have always served Epping Station, latterly providing interchange at the eastern end of London Underground's Central Line. For many years, buses on route 339 (Harlow to Brentwood and Warley via Epping and Ongar) double-ran through Epping town in order to serve it. RML2352 (HA) does so on 3rd June 1977, during its brief period of RML operation. Today, part of the 339 has been revived using RT and RM-type buses to link this station with the Epping Ongar Heritage Railway.

Another station where local routes were diverted off their main line of route to serve it was St. Albans City, on the Midland Main Line. The station is in the throes of reconstruction as RMC1517 (HF) calls there on its way to Hertford on the busy 341 on 18th October 1977, shortly before this route converted to O.P.O. Today, this station is busier than ever thanks to Thameslink serving it.

MARKET DAY

Many of the towns served by London's Country buses and Green Line coaches had bustling markets. Typical was St. Albans, where market stalls line both sides of St. Peters Street in the city centre. The oddly-liveried RT3081 (LS) passes through on the 321's long journey to Luton on a gloomy 20th January 1968.

A week later, on 27th January 1968, RF207 (NF) passes through Bromley Market Place on the southern peripheral Green Line route 725 on its way to Windsor. As may be seen by the conductor standing at the front of the RF on the nearside, this route was still crew-operated at the time. Interestingly, it was also possible to travel from Bromley to Windsor on Green Line routes 704 and 705 at this time - these travelled through Central London rather that the south London suburbs.

Hertford is a busy market town, and its market place was adjacent to the bus station in the 1960s and 1970s. RFs dominated it when downgraded ex-Green Line RF86 (HG) arrived there on local route 333B on 30th March 1968.

Hatfield also had its market in the more modern part of the town fifty or so years ago. On 27th April 1968, RT4740 (HF) on local route 340A which served Hatfield and Welwyn Garden City, hurries past on its way to Hatfield Station.

Back in St. Albans on the same day, RF229 (SA) - another RF downgraded from Green Line coach to bus status in the mid-1960s and now looking somewhat shoddy - passes through the market area with a good load of passengers on route 355, which linked Borehamwood and Harpenden.

Enfield Town's historic market square dates back make many centuries. On 29th June 1968, RF286 (SA) - another former Green Line coach - has just terminated there on route 313, and will run around the block to stand in Cecil Road before returning to St. Albans. As related earlier, this route still exists as a London Buses service linking Potters Bar and Chingford via Enfield.

Above: Like Enfield, Dartford's market place was graced by trolleybuses for twenty-odd years. By 6th July 1968, when RT3054 (DT) loads up with shoppers on local route 491, they had long been replaced there by red bus route 96 - which still serves the town today. Sadly, however, the many Country bus and Green Line coach routes which served the town in the 1960s and 1970s are now but a distant memory!

Left: Subbing for one of the RMLs which replaced RTs on routes 347 and 347A in the spring of 1966, RT3147 (HH) sets off from Watford's busy market place for who knows where on 13th July 1968. Presumably its conductor told its passengers where it was going!

Above: Epping is another market town on the edge of Greater London, whose market stalls are strung along its historic High Street. On 5th September, ex-Green Line RF269 (HA) sets collects shoppers who have walked around the corner by the parish church to board local route 381 for Toothill. Part of this route has been revived in recent years in connection with the Epping Ongar Railway, bringing RFs back to the town.

Right: The market and shopping centre of Stevenage New Town is situated conveniently adjacent to the bus station, where on 28th April 1972, shoppers clamber aboard RT4105 (SV) bound for St. Nicholas. It contrasts with an SM the Superbus service, which had replaced RTs on the original route 809 to Chells.

The old-established market town of Romford is also on the edge of Greater London. Originally, its many bus routes ran through the centre of the street market area, but in the late 1960s, a new ring-road around it was created avoiding this. On 2nd June 1973, shoppers fill up RP48 (RE) on the northern orbital Green Line route 724, whose western terminus had now become Staines rather than High Wycombe. A red RT on route 193 bound for Barking is about to overtake it.

OLD ORDER

Between 1954 and the end of London Transport Country Area bus and Green Line coach operation, rigid standardisation meant that RTs and RFs dominated the fleet. This view at Harlow Bus Station on 6th April 1968 typifies that, albeit RF112 (HA) on route 720 had been modernised a year or so previously. RT577 (HA) on route 397 heading for one of LT's northernmost outposts, Bishops Stortford, was the lowest numbered post-war RT ever to operate in Country Area green livery, being one of the formerly red RT3/1-bodied RTs overhauled in green in 1963/64. The earliest numbered post-war RT delivered in green was RT597; RT593 preserved in Country Area livery today was always a red bus when in service.

RFs typified both the Green Line coach and Country bus single-deck fleets from 1952, right through until the early years of London Country twenty years later. Many Green Line coaches were demoted to bus status in the mid-1960s, becoming identical in outward appearance to those that had always been buses, other than still keeping the brackets for their Green Line route side-boards. RF247 (WR), however, has had these removed when heading through Slough on local route 460 on 8th March 1969.

Typifying Country RFs which had always been buses, RF700 (GR) arrives at Rickmansworth Station on local route 309A on 2nd July 1969. There were 700 RFs in all - thus this one was the highest-numbered. Those originally delivered as Country buses had matching registration numbers.

This scene at a very wet Sevenoaks Bus Station on 25th October 1969 typifies the final years of the "old order" of the London Transport Country bus and Green Line coach fleet. RF634 (DS) and RCL2260 (WR) stand there two months before their transfer to London Country. The RF has a later style of front blind, whereas the RCL bears the later LT Green Line coach livery adopted for the RMCs and RCLs upon overhaul and repaint in 1967/68.

For the first two or three years of London Country operation, the old order still prevailed in many instances. This is typified by RT4107 (HH) changing crew opposite Two Waters Garage on 4th October 1972. Aside from gaining the L.C.B.S. "flying polo" emblem on the stairwell, a London Country fleet name on its side, and its LT radiator badge removed, the RT is still in LT Country Area livery. The bus and coach stop, too, is still an LT one - complete with red and green finials above it denoting that both Country bus and Green Line coaches serve it - but all was soon due to change!

Aside from the LT "bullseye" missing from the front of modernised Green Line coach RF281 (WY), this scene at Marble Arch could be in the late 1960s. However, I took it on 1st September 1976, by which time the chance of seeing "old order" RFs and RTs on Green Line service was very remote indeed. However the questionable performance of the RPs on route 716 meant that RFs had to be used as back-up for them, whereas the appearance of RT3530 (TG) on a regular evening rush hour turn on the 706 resulted from the poor performance of Leyland Nationals on that route!

NEW ORDER

Although the SM class of vehicles had been ordered by London Transport, the adornment of some of them at Stevenage for the new New Town "Superbus" service which replaced route 809 between the Bus Station and Chells in a striking blue and yellow livery somehow heralded the "new order" being imposed by London Country. What a shame these A.E.C. Swifts proved to be such a disaster in both London Transport and London Country service.

Another obvious sign of change was the downgrading of the RMC and RCL class Routemaster Green Line coaches to bus status between December 1971 and May 1972. This led to them being given London Country fleetnames and stairwell symbols in yellow, along with matching waistbands, and also external adverts which Green Line coaches never had. On 1st September 1972, RMC1488 (SJ) illustrates their new status when circumnavigating the roundabout at Orpington War Memorial on route 477, but has yet to receive external advertising.

Modernised Green Line coach RFs received the London Country "flying polo" symbol in place of the London Transport "bullseye" on the front, and this symbol also replaced LT "bullseyes" at bus stations and garages - as it has done above the enquiry office at Hemel Hempstead Bus Station, visible on the right. RF130, still in Green Line livery, is being used as a bus there on 4th October 1972, with a somewhat confusing blind display for route 307. Usually, by this time, RFs' blind-boxes were masked to allow room for more of these narrower displays.

The ninety-strong RP class of Park Royal-bodied A.E.C. Reliance Green Line coaches delivered to London Country in late 1971 and early 1972 had the same two-tone green livery as modernised RFs, complete with the L.C.B.S. symbol at the front. Most replaced RMCs and RCLs, but they also deputised for RFs on such routes as the 701 and 702. On 25th May 1973, RP42 (ST) awaits departure from Victoria, Eccleston Bridge, on the latter.

By early 1973, London Country had imposed on it the National Bus Company diktat that all of their buses must bear one of their standard corporate liveries, in this case leaf green, as well as standardised fleet names bearing the N.B.C. symbol. Their RMLs were due for overhaul at this period, but not all of them received a full overhaul and thus some still retained the older Lincoln green livery. One that did gain the N.B.C. style was RML2429 (GR), which passes Bushey and Oxhey Station on 10th April 1975. Is it a 306 or a 306A? The use of a canopy blind in its front number box confuses all and sundry!

A more drastic change from London Transport policy was the large-scale introduction into the London Country fleet of Leyland Nationals. Many of the earliest were used as Green Line coaches, adorned in the N.B.C.'s green and white dual-purpose livery. On 29th September 1975, SNC129 (NF) on route 701 is on diversion at the junction of Pont Street and Sloane Street, owing to the famous Spaghetti House Siege in Knightsbridge, an armed robbery that went wrong (for the robbers, that is!).

The imposition of N.B.C. corporate livery extended to RFs, which thanks to their reliability and ability to be used on virtually any route survived much longer than intended owing to the dismal failure of newer types such as the MB and SM. It did not suit them, as this view of RF690 (GY) at the Uplands Estate terminus of route 374 on 28th February 1976 shows!

A surprise, however, was the appearance of three late-surviving RTs (RT604, 1018 and 3461) at Chelsham Garage in the early summer of 1977 in full N.B.C. corporate livery. The latter of these heads through South End, Croydon on 28th June 1977. Oddly, they only lasted in service for a few months in this guise, though all three were later preserved. Of them, only RT604 makes regular appearances at rallies and running days today.

By the beginning of 1980, the Green Line network had been radically revised, mainly with long cross-London routes inherited from London Transport being split into two halves to combat traffic congestion. Thus a new Green Line express route 710 appeared, running between London and Guildford, largely via the Kingston By-Pass. Bearing a revised dual-purpose livery, RP70(GF) passes Marble Arch on 29th February 1980.

At the same period, large numbers of Leyland Nationals were entering the London Country fleet (as they also were by now with London Transport). These saw off earlier double- and single-deckers alike. On 1st March 1980, SNB267 (HA) represents the new order on route 339 at Epping Station. The RF behind is on an enthusiasts' tour.

Efforts were also made at this period to improve the image of Green Line coach services by introducing luxury coaches to them, rather than the dual-purpose vehicles used hitherto (as RF, RMC, RCL and RP class "coaches" really were). Most were Duple or Plaxton-bodied A.E.C. Reliances, but two Duple-bodied Volvo's were also tried. One of them, DV1 (WY) calls at Turnpike Lane Station on 20th April 1980 on route 734. This had been introduced a few months previously following the old 715 route from Hertford via Enfield to Wood Green, then travelling via such places as Muswell Hill, Brent Cross and Heathrow Airport to Addlestone. Unfortunately, its long and winding route was sabotaged by traffic congestion!

Another reason why Green Line's fortunes declined at this time was that the new Leyland National "coaches" which replaced RFs on such routes as the 708 were unpopular with passengers, not least thanks to their awful plastic seats. Typical is SNC194 which is already well past its best when passing Hyde Park Corner on that route in July 1980.

Apart from the XF class Daimler Fleetlines inherited from London Transport, the eleven AF class Fleetlines with Northern Counties bodywork were London Country's first O.M.O. double-deckers, delivered early in 1972 and a diverted order from fellow-N.B.C. company Western Welsh. They were allocated to Godstone Garage to replace RMLs on route 410, later appearing on the 409 and 411, on which AF8 (GD) arrives at the Garage in April 1982. By now, being non-standard, some had already been withdrawn. London Country had standardised on the Leyland Atlantean instead.

Some of London Country's early Leyland Nationals of the longer LNB variety did not last too long either, but on 22nd April 1982, LNB40 (RG) calls at Sutton Station on new route 422, which largely replaced the outer section of Green Line route 711. It passes London Transport's locally-based DMS191, itself not much longer of this world!

Nicely illustrating London Country's single-deck fleet at this time, RP11 (SA) escorts a Leyland National along St. Peters Street, St. Albans also in April 1982. By now, RPs were being withdrawn and this one has been demoted to bus status, despite retaining Green Line livery.

In London Country's final years before being split up as a prelude to privatisation, its network of Green Line coach routes was further revised, with some protruding beyond the former London Transport area. An example was the 740 which ran from Victoria to Farnham via Guildford, on which RP18 (GF) approaches Hyde Park Corner on 9th July 1982.

The same RP as in the previous picture has become a 741 upon arrival at Victoria, and now sets off for Whitehill when heading along Ebury Street. A strike by British Rail staff has increased demand for Green Line services for a few days, perhaps giving the RPs a "last fling".

ALL-OVER ADVERTS

In common with London Transport, London Country indulged in the all-over advertisement fad of the early 1970s. One of the most lurid examples was the livery given to RP46 (DG) which crosses Lambeth Bridge on route 705 on 12th April 1973. This was for Wimpy Bars and carried a basically glaring orange livery: only the small area surrounding its Green Line fleet name was green!

RMC1516 (HF) was adorned in an all-over advertisement livery for the Welwyn Department Store, and usually ran on busy route 341 between St. Albans and Hertford, in whose bus station it stands on 26th April 1973. One of the first RFs to be given N.B.C. corporate livery noses in on the left.

RP87 (HA) was another of its class to carry all-over advertising, in this case for Airfix Construction Kits. On 31st March 1974, it climbs Goldings Hill out of Loughton into Epping Forest on its way to Harlow on route 718.

Somewhat appropriately advertising colour television by Rediffusion, Atlantean AN7 (SV), one of the first of its class which had replaced RTs on Stevenage New Town services just over two years previously, stands in Stevenage Bus Station on 6th November 1974. Routes 813 and 814 had been introduced to replace the complicated 800 and 801 series of routes at that time. Immediately behind the AN on the left may be seen Stevenage Garage, very conveniently situated adjacent to the bus station, despite which it was closed in 1991.

Even one of the ill-fated SMs in London Country's fleet received an all-over advertisement. This was SM476 (MA), which looked quite attractive in a basically dark blue and white livery promoting the Buckinghamshire Advertiser newspaper. On 22nd April 1975, it heads along Chesham High Street on the long 353 route from Amersham to Windsor.

RMC1490 (GY) was another of its class to carry an all-over advert, in a basically white livery for London & Manchester Assurance. Originally adorned in a different style to that shown here and operated from Reigate Garage in 1973, by 1st April 1976 it had moved to Grays, from where it is working local route 375 at Stonehouse Corner. However, it returned to Reigate a few weeks later.

Not strictly an all-over advert, but a "wrap-around", is carried by AN105 (HG) when working local route 395 at Hertford North Station on 17th May 1980. Fishpools is a department store at Waltham Cross, which this AN would have passed when working route 310 between Hertford and Enfield.

BORDERLANDS

Inevitably, Country Area bus routes intruded into the Central Area around the periphery of Greater London. Uxbridge Bus Station was a place where several Country routes terminated, arriving from Berkshire, Buckinghamshire and Hertfordshire. From the latter RT3027 (GR) awaits departure on 28th September 1966 on route 347 with a very uninformative blind display indeed! Perhaps this is because it is subbing for an RML, which type had replaced RTs on the 347 and 347A (which ran to Watford and Hemel Hempstead) in the spring of that year.

For many years, trunk routes 310 and 310A from Hertford and Hoddesdon ran to Enfield Town. On 20th April 1968, RT750 (HG) - one of the ex-red RT3/1-bodied RTs - arrives there with its destination blind already set for its return to Hertford. In recent times, the 310 and its derivatives have been truncated at the border between the former Central and Country Areas at Waltham Cross: absurdly, no London bus routes cross the border into Hertfordshire and Essex there as they once did, either: all passengers have to change buses at Waltham Cross Bus Station!

Many CountryArea trunk routes penetrated well into the Central Area to terminate in Croydon. On a wet 2nd May 1968, RT598 (DS) has just set off from West Croydon on its long trek to Horsham via Dorking. Then, routes 403, 405, 408, 409, 411, 414 and 470 radiated from West Croydon, heading for Tonbridge, Horsham via Crawley, Guildford, Forest Row, Reigate (via Godstone), Horsham via Dorking and Dorking (via Leatherhead) respectively. Today, only the much-truncated 403 and 405 remain - both are now London Buses routes.

In the East, trunk route 370 penetrated well into the Central Area, reaching Romford. On 18th May 1968, RT2630 (GY), another ex-red RT with an RT3/1 body, loads up at Romford Station. Today, this route too still exists as a London Buses service.

Left: Back at Uxbridge, RT3251 (HE) awaits departure on a short working of route 305 on 1st June 1968. It still bears Green Line livery, having been displaced by RCLs at Romford London Road Garage some three years previously. For some reason, a number of former Green Line RTs which had been at Romford were based at Amersham and High Wycombe Garages at this period. This one, which had returned to London Transport in 1972 and lasted until the end of RT operation at Barking in 1979, is now part of the Ensignbus Heritage Fleet.

Country Area routes 401 and 486 penetrated the Central Area in the Bexleyheath area, oddly serving roads that red buses did not! On 6th July 1968, ex-red RT3/1-bodied RT1140 (SJ) heads for Belvedere Station at Bexleyheath Clock Tower.

Somewhat curiously, Potters Bar is outside Great London proper, yet had a Central Area bus garage and was served by several Central Area routes, as indeed it still has today. However, several Country Area routes passed through the town. Two were the long 303 and 303A trunk routes; on 15th October 1968, RT3897 (HF) waits at the traffic lights by The White Lion pub in Potters Bar High Street on the latter.

The second Country Area route to serve Belvedere and Bexleyheath was the 486, on which RF584 (DT) negotiates the one-way system in Bexleyheath town centre on 20th September 1969. A much-altered London Buses route 486 still serves this area today.

On the same day as the previous picture, RT967 (DT) heads past The Barley Mow in Foots Cray High Street. Route 467 was at this time the only Country Area route to penetrate as far into this part of the Central Area, terminating at Sidcup Station.

Country Area routes 402 and 410 reached as far as Bromley North Station. Also on 20th September 1969, RT3454 (RG) passes through Bromley Market Place heading back to is home town on the latter route. It has been working as an extra for the Biggin Hill Air Display; the 410 had converted to RML operation four years previously.

On 6th July 1971, RF652 (DG) approaches Bromley South Station bound for Sevenoaks on route 402. Of note is the restricted blind display, necessary because the RFs at Dunton Green Garage worked a large number of routes with varying destinations.

Trunk routes 403, 408 and 470 all skirted the southern edge of the Central Area between Croydon and Wallington, the latter two continuing to Cheam. On 16th June 1972, RT611 (LH) passes Carshalton Ponds on a short working of route 408 to Effingham.

On the same day, a balding RT4031 (LH) passes through Sutton town centre on sister route 470 bound for Dorking. Both the 408 and 470 converted to AN O.M.O. next day.

Country Area routes 406, 406A and 418 reached Kingston-Upon-Thames, where they terminated adjacent to the Southern Region railway station. Also on 16th June 1972, RT2504 (LH) runs around the one-way system in the town centre. Although route 406 converted to RMC operation the following year, RTs still appeared on it as late as the early part of 1978.

In addition to routes 303, 303A and 340B which started at New Barnet and headed to Hatfield, Welwyn and beyond, Potters Bar was also served by routes 350 and 350A. These also came from New Barnet and then meandered through the Hertfordshire countryside all the way to Bishops Stortford. On 21st March 1973, ex-Green Line RF71 (HG) is only however going as far as Hertford. It calls in the busy lay-by outside Potters Bar Garage. Today, the gardens in front of the garage, visible on the right, have been paved over to provide extra parking space for Potters Bar's buses, more than 200 of them are based there nowadays.

Whereas route 370 from Tilbury and Grays reached Romford, other routes from that area intruded on the Central Area as far as Rainham. On 2nd June 1973, RF189 (GY), another downgraded from Green Line coach status in the mid-1960s, stands at route 371's Rainham Church terminus, bound for Tilbury. On the right, two red RMLs on route 165 have also terminated there.

Although Epsom is outside Greater London proper, it was served both by London Transport Central Area and Country Area/London Country buses in the 1960s and 1970s. On 5th June 1974, downgraded modernised Green Line RF213 (LH) heads along East Road out of the town centre bound for Chessington Zoo on "cross-border" route 468. I took this picture from the front upper deck seat of a DMS stuck in traffic heading for Derby Day on red bus route 293!

Borehamwood is also just outside Greater London, but was (and still is) served by red London buses. A number of Country routes however reached the town from the north, one being the 358 from St. Albans. On 6th November 1975, SMW10 (SA) heads along Furzehill Road, Borehamwood. This is one of the second of two batches of A.E.C. Swifts transferred from South Wales Transport in 1971, all this batch with Marshall single-door bodywork were allocated to St. Albans throughout their lives with London Country. They lasted until 1981, when most of the indigenous SMs were also finally withdrawn.

As mentioned previously much of Country route 403 ran within the Central Area. The entire section between Croydon and Wallington, which no longer runs today, did so, and on this, RMC1487 (CM) turns from Purley Way into Waddon Road on 11th October 1978, shortly before the main service on route 403 converted to O.P.O. Despite being acquired by London Transport and actually painted red for use as a driver trainer, it was never used by them and sold privately for preservation in 1981. I was a co-owner of it between 1984 and 1987.

ODDITIES

Inevitably, the Country Area/London Country and Green Line fleets included a number of odd vehicles, and also operated unusual routes. Working in place of one of the scheduled RC class coaches on their last day of operation on route 705, 29th November 1967, RF136 (DS) calls at Hyde Park Corner on its way to Sevenoaks. This RF is unique, being the prototype modernised Green Line RF. Converted as such in the spring of 1966, it was given RT-style mudguards instead of retaining its originals, which all other RFs kept upon modernisation. It was subsequently preserved.

Whereas all other Country Area routes numbered in the 800 series served new towns, route 803 was an Express service which ran from Uxbridge to Welwyn Garden City, via Watford, St. Albans and Hatfield. On 14th May 1968, a very well-filled RT4726 (GR) speeds along Rickmansworth High Street. Curiously, an express service between West Croydon and Chelsham on route 403 was not given a separate number, though both had LT's standard blue via blinds as used for express services.

Originally, all Country bus RFs had matching registration and stock-numbers. However, in 1953/54, the first three examples converted to one-man operation were renumbered, thus RF649 (HH) became RF699. On a cold and dismal 14th February 1969, it calls at The Marlowes in Hemel Hempstead New Town on rural route 307 which linked Harpenden with Redbourn. Needless to say although later all Country bus RFs were quickly converted to O.M.O. in the latter half of the 1950s, those that had been renumbered were not given their original numbers back!

The nationwide vehicle spares shortage of the mid-1970s caused many unscheduled vehicle type-to-route workings with both London Transport and London Country. Elderly RTs in particular appeared on routes normally operated by Routemasters, or even in London Country's case O.P.O. types. On 19th June 1973, RT4046 (ST) heads along Church Street, Staines standing in for an RML. It also has an RML side-blind in its front via box. In the event, some of London Country's RMLs which were kaput at this time never ran again and went for scrap at the end of 1977.

One of the most extreme cases of odd workings on London Country services at this period was that of modernised Green Line RF70 (TG) subbing for an RMC on trunk route 301 between Aylesbury and Little Bushey on 30th April 1975. Followed by a red MB on route 258, it turns from Chalk Hill into Aldenham Road, Bushey and despite the "pay as you enter" notice, also has a conductor on board!

For more than three years after they were replaced on most of the Stevenage New Town routes by ANs, three RTs remained at Stevenage Garage to work rush hour and Sunday journeys on routes 303 and 303C between Stevenage and Hitchin. This was due to the bridge carrying the Great Northern main line above the old Great North Road at Little Wymondley being too low for an AN to pass beneath. On 2nd May 1975, RT603 (SV) contrasts with an AN and two SMs in Stevenage Bus Station. It is also overheating, and carries an improvised blind display.

Some of the oddest vehicles ever operated by London Country were three Northern Counties-bodied full-fronted Leyland Titan PD3s transferred from Southdown. Nicknamed "Queen Mary's" and dating from 1958, they retained Southdown's smart light green and cream livery (albeit with London Country fleet-names) even though they ran alongside Southdown vehicles at route 409's southern extremity between East Grinstead and Forest Row! They were bought to assist the shortage of RMLs, and lasted just over a year. On 9th October 1975, LS2 (GD) heads into Croydon along South End.

Even though route 409 had received RMLs in replacement of its RTs in the autumn of 1965, more than ten years later RTs still made odd appearances on it. Also heading for West Croydon, RT4742 (RG) heads through Old Coulsdon, passing The Tudor Rose pub, on 17th October 1975.

Although three RCLs were retained at Godstone Garage for route 709 for some four years after all the others were demoted to bus status, only one of them received corporate N.B.C. livery and a Green Line fleet-name, thus making it unique. This was RCL2237 (GD) which passes the junction of Kennington Road and Kennington Lane on the very last (officially) crew-operated trip on the 709, back to Godstone, on 14th May 1976. Balloons inside it and a banner in the RCL's lower-deck nearside front window may just be discerned commemorating this.

At a time when Green Line route 706 was usually operated by SNC class Leyland Nationals, a remarkable evening rush hour working from Aylesbury to Victoria and back on it for several days in the late summer of 1976 was that of RT3530 (TG), recalling the "good old days" of RTs working Green Line reliefs! On 3rd September 1976, it calls at Marble Arch on its way north, complete with correctly set Green Line blinds. Whether this was the last instance of an RT working a Green Line service I unfortunately no longer recall.

Oddities in the London Country fleet were fourteen SMW class A.E.C. Swifts acquired from South Wales Transport when fairly new in 1971. The first three had Willowbrook dual-door bodies, the remainder Marshall bodies with a single entrance/exit. On 18th October 1977, SMW10 (SA) heads along Victoria Street out of St. Albans, bound for Brookmans Park on route 343.

Just as RTs and RFs did, London Country Routemasters were allocated to various garages towards the end of their service with them to cover for missing O.P.O. types. One was RML2354 (HG) which heads along Ware Road, Hertford subbing for an AN on route 316 on 10th November 1977. This route had never been officially crew-operated, having been renumbered from 310A when converted to O.M.O.

Another bizarre use of RMLs late in their London Country lives that that of those based at Harlow for route 339 being used on new Green Line routes 702 and 703 in place of the scheduled RPs. On the former, which had replaced the 718 between Walthamstow and Harlow, a shabby RML2352 (HA) heads south along Chingford Road on a wet 21st April 1978.

Another instance of secondhand vehicles being acquired by London Country was that of the Plaxton-bodied RN-class A.E.C. Reliances. New in 1971 to the well-known independent operator Barton of Nottingham, ten of them were bought in 1977. Despite their "Panorama" coach bodies, they had two-and-three seating, cramming 64 passengers into them and were used as buses, although London Country downseated them to "only" 60! Usually used on local bus routes and school contracts at Dorking and Leatherhead Garages, they also found their way onto Green Line route 714. RN10 (DS) works this at Hammersmith, Butterwick on 24th February 1979.

Another one-off class in the London Country fleet was the SMAs. There were 21 of these Alexander-bodied A.E.C. Swifts, which were a diverted order from South Wales Transport. They were kitted out as Green Line coaches and most were used on southern orbital route 725, though one of them, SMW20 (NF) spent most of its life working as a private hire coach at Crawley. However, late in its life it moved to Northfleet from where it works the 726 (a derivative of the 725, which still exists today as a London Buses route) through Dartford on 1st October 1979. It was one of few of the class to gain N.B.C. corporate Green Line livery. Underpowered like the main SM class, the SMAs lasted less than a decade in service.

GREEN LINE ACROSS LONDON

By the mid-1960s, the Green Line coach network had changed little since that re-established after the war, most of them running across London. Many of the routes still had the RFs allocated to them which replaced pre-war types in 1951/52, too. On 11th July 1967, Country bus RF611 (CM) speeds through Edgware on the long 706, which ran from Westerham to Aylesbury. At this time, it was still crew-operated and its conductor may be seen standing to the right of the driver.

RFs on several busy routes were replaced by new RMC class Routemaster coaches in 1962/63. One was the 717 , upon which RMC1494 (HF) arrives at Golders Green Station on its journey from Welwyn Garden City to Wrotham on 19th November 1967, shortly before the route was withdrawn north of Baker Street and reverted to RF operation. The RMC is still in original condition, but will soon receive its first overhaul, too.

A week later, on 26th November 1967, modernised RF107 (TG) speeds along Croydon High Street on its way from Aylesbury to Oxted on route 707, which would be withdrawn in February 1969. Much of it paralleled routes 706 and 708. At this time, the routes were still crew-operated - the conductor stands in this RF's front nearside.

Inevitably, RFs which had been downgraded from Green Line coach to Country bus status frequently found their way back onto Green Line routes. This has happened to RF199 (DS), again crew-operated, calling at Hammersmith Butterwick on its way from Luton to Dorking on the 714 on 27th December 1967.

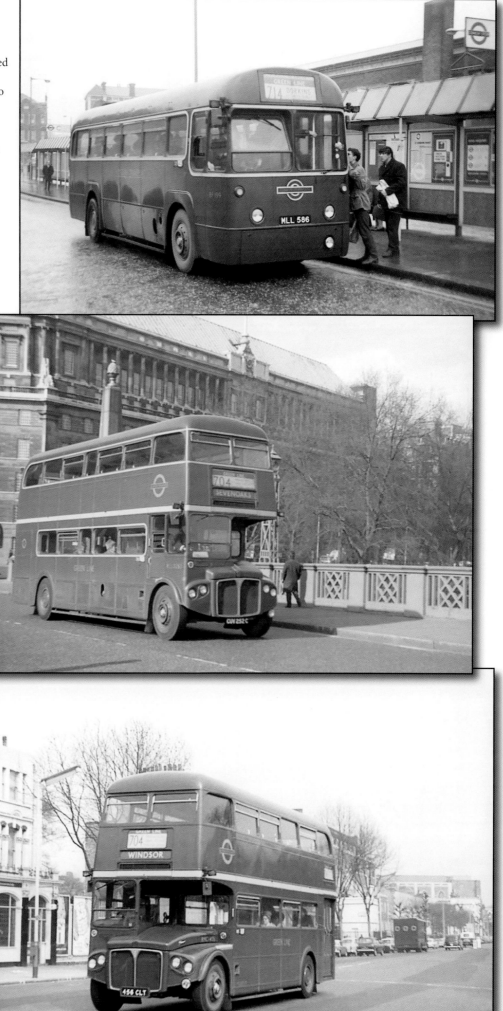

Most of the forty-three RCL class long Routemaster coaches began life in the summer of 1965 replacing RTs on routes that connected Aldgate with south-west Essex. However, by 5th March 1968, reductions in these routes, had released sufficient of them to operate routes 704 and 705, both of which started at Windsor, and crossed London to finish at Tunbridge Wells and Sevenoaks respectively. On that date, RCL2252 (DG) crosses Lambeth Bridge on an apparently truncated 704 working. It is still in its original livery, which upon repaint was revised to omit the light green window surrounds.

While the RCLs were undergoing their first intermediate repaints, a couple of RMCs covered for them on routes 704 and 705. On 9th April 1968, RMC1456 (WR) passes the Imperial War Museum bearing the new livery RMCs received on overhaul in 1967/68, which the RCLs were also receiving. Windsor Garage had RMCs anyway for their share of route 718.

Route 710 ran from Crawley to Chesham, but was withdrawn north of Baker Street late in 1968, then subsequently restricted to running only between Uxbridge and Amersham before complete withdrawal in 1972. On 15th July 1968, RF143 (GM) speeds past Streatham Common on its way north. This RF was based at Victoria, Gillingham Street Garage as a spare to cover for any breakdowns suffered by Green Line coaches in Central London. It has a restricted blind display to accommodate a special one-line blind that included most Green Line routes and their destinations.

Further south along the Brighton Road, downgraded ex-Green Line RF41 (EG) hurries past Thornton Heath Pond on 1st March 1969, on route 708's long journey from Hemel Hempstead to East Grinstead. Just over a fortnight before, the route had been converted from RMC back to RF operation, becoming O.M.O. too.

Green Line routes 712 and 713 both linked Dorking with Luton and Dunstable, though had differing routeings in the St. Albans area. On 25th March 1970, RF118 (DS), still sporting an LT "bullseye" nearly four months after being taken over by London Country, speeds southwards through Cheam.

The version of route 715A which ran when the RMCs on parent route 715 were replaced by RPs in the spring of 1972 ran only on Saturdays, linking Guildford and Hertford via Kingston town centre, rather than via the Kingston By-Pass as the 715 did. On its last day of RMC operation, 22nd April 1972, RMC1474 (GF) passes the Church and Convent of the Blessed Mother Maria of Majdanek in Camden Town.

Route 711, linking High Wycombe and Reigate, was well known for being host to various experimental types of Green Line coach over the years, but on 28th March 1973, there is nothing special about modernised RF135 (RG) other than its recently having been downgraded to bus status and given a yellow waistband. It stands at the traffic lights by Oval Station, heading south.

Still in Green Line livery but lacking a front "flying polo" emblem, RF38 (SJ) has just called at Lewisham Odeon on its way from Wrotham to Hemel Hempstead on 14th April 1973. Route 719 originally terminated at Victoria from the north, but was extended late in 1968 to replace the withdrawn 717 down to Wrotham in Kent.

By the spring of 1974, RF164 (GF) was outstationed at London Transport's Riverside Garage to cover for any Green Line coaches that broke down on routes serving west or south-west London that did not serve Victoria. On 14th April that year, one of the troublesome RPs on route 716 must have broken down, since it finds itself on that route's long trek from Chertsey to Hitchin when passing Barnet Church. In common with the emergency RF at Gillingham Street, it has a restricted blind display for one-line blinds showing many different destinations.

Routes 715 and 715A had been the first to convert from RF to RMC operation (in August 1962), and then received RPs in April 1972. However probably owing to the latters' questionable performance, RF's could often be seen working it long after they officially did. Thus on 28th May 1974, RF240 (HG), one that had been downgraded from Green Line coach to Country Bus status in the mid-1960s, passes Palmers Green Triangle on its journey from Guildford to Hertford. The lack of passengers illustrates the decline in Green Line's fortunes by this time.

By late 1974, the only Green Line route to retain a full RF allocation was the 706, Leyland Nationals having recently taken over such routes as the 708, 712, 713 and 714. However at this time of the chronic vehicle spares shortage, RFs were kept at most garages to cover for other types, and on 10th December 1974, modernised RF26 (DS) passes Hendon Central Station on the way from Dunstable to Dorking on the 712. It is unusually painted in NBC leaf green, but with a white waistband. Numerically, this was the pioneer Green Line RF and was subsequently preserved.

Another modernised RF downgraded to bus status, RF85 (MA) is on loan to Garston Garage when subbing for an SNC on route 719 on 24th February 1975. It climbs Sidcup Hill on the way from Wrotham to Hemel Hempstead.

Not surprisingly, RFs still appeared on route 706 after its final conversion to SNC operation. On 11th September 1975, ex-coach RF221 (CM) has a long way to go to reach Aylebsury when heading along Sussex Road, South Croydon.

Following the original 716's withdrawal in the spring of 1976, the 716A (whose southern terminus had been Woking rather than Cherstsey) was renumbered 716. On 31st July 1977, RP52 (WY) in the N.B.C. corporate Green Line livery has called at Golders Green Station on its way from Hitchin to Woking.

Also bearing the later livery, RP26 (GF) calls at Turnpike Lane Station on a rainy 26th October 1979 on the 715's trek from Guildford to Hertford. Not long afterwards. the route was cut in half, with the northern section renumbered 735. This was a fate that befell most Green Line routes in later years, effectively ending their traditional cross-London operation.

ALL HANDS ON DECK!

The spare parts shortage which afflicted both London Transport and London Country in the mid-1970s has already been mentioned in these pages. Fortunately for London Country, London Transport had dozens of unwanted MBs and MBSs on its hands, which were willingly accepted on loan by them to help out. On 19th April 1975, a dented MBS54 (GR) heads along Clarendon Road, Watford on route 318. The country lanes this route served were a far cry from the back streets of Wood Green and Hornsey where it had originally run!

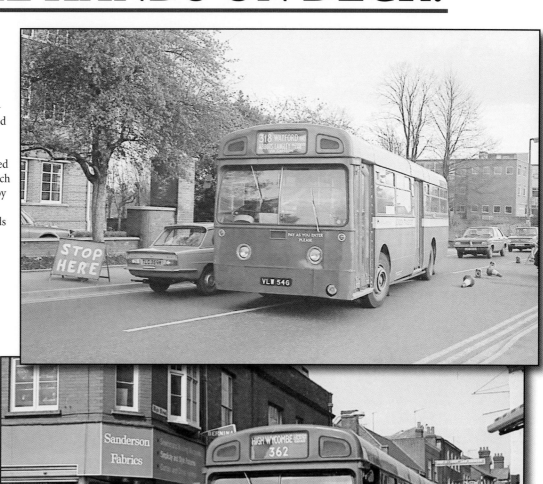

The red MB-types on loan to London Country were spread far and wide; 50-seat conventional O.M.O. MB145 (HE) was sent to distant High Wycombe Garage, from which it works route 362 along Chesham High Street on 22nd April 1975.

Another 50-seat MB, MB149 (GR) is working local route 346, when passing the remains of the old Watford High Street Garage on 30th April 1975. These red buses in Watford must have confused passengers at the time, since red MBs on route 258 and red SMSs on route 142 served the same roads!

Left: On Derby Day in 1974, racegoers' route 406F was largely operated by red MB-types on loan to London Country. Just one of them worked it the following year, MB160 (LH), the last of the batch of 50-seaters. On 4th June 1975, it is pursued along Ashley Road, Epsom by XF1 on the same route.

Below: Back in the Watford area, a battered MB132 (GR) approaches Garston Garage on local route 352 on 16th July 1975. After a year or so on loan to London Country, most of these unfortunate vehicles went for scrap.

As London Country's vehicle spares shortage worsened, and the certificates of fitness on most of the London Transport MB-types on loan to them expired, more extreme measures had to be resorted to - literally a case of "all hands on deck". Buses from other operators began to be hired, some of the first being sent to Dartford Garage from nearby Maidstone Corporation. These were Massey-bodied Leyland Titan PD2's in light blue and cream livery. No.14 heads along Hythe Street, Dartford on 28th February 1976 on route 499, whose RMCs were dispersed to cover shortages elsewhere.

At the same period, route 477's RMCs at Swanley Garage were replaced by East Lancs-bodied A.E.C. Regent V's loaned from Eastbourne Corporation. This lucky shot in the yard of Dartford Garage, also on 28th February 1976, catches their No.67, in its smart cream and dark blue livery, with two Maidstone Corporation Leyland PD2s.

The next operator to loan buses to London Country was Southend Corporation. These were Leyland Titan PD3s with Massey and Northern Counties bodywork which had recently been hired to London Transport and used on route 190 from South Croydon Garage. Their new home was Harlow, where they replaced RTs on route 339. On 9th April 1976, Southend No.335 of the 1965 Massey-bodied batch passes Brentwood, Robin Hood & Little John on its way to Harlow. Livery is light blue and cream.

A third seaside town to loan buses to London Country was Bournemouth. In addition to double-deck Daimler Fleetlines based at Leatherhead Garage for routes 408 and 470, some unusual Daimler Roadliner single-deckers worked from Staines Garage, which their No.53 has just left for a trip to Slough on route 460 on 15th May 1976.

On a hot, sunny 8th June 1976, Eastbourne Corporation Regent V No.67 (SJ) approaches Orpington War Memorial on route 477. It should have been more at home with its seaside operator in that hot, dry summer!

Maidstone Corporation again came to London Country's aid in 1977, when some of their Massey-bodied Leyland Atlanteans were sent to Chelsham Garage, and ran alongside the three N.B.C. corporate-liveried RTs on route 403. On 28th June 1977, No.28 of the 1965 batch, heads along South End, Croydon on a short working to West Croydon.

EAST END

Most of the Green Line routes linking London with south-west Essex did not run through Central London, but terminated at Aldgate, Minories Bus and Green Line Coach Station. The exception was route 718. On 6th January 1968, modernised Green Line RF246 (HA) heads into town through Stratford Broadway on route 720, which travelled via Epping and Harlow to Bishops Stortford. Along with the now-withdrawn sister route 720A, it had had RMCs briefly, but soon reverted to RF operation.

Another of the Aldgate Green Line routes was the 722, which somewhat oddly ran entirely within the Central Area, terminating at Upminster, Corbetts Tey, although for a few months was extended through the Dartford Tunnel to Dartford itself. One of Romford London Road's RT-operated routes, it converted to RCL in 1965, but two years later reverted to RT using those in Green Line livery hitherto used for relief duties. One of these, RT999 (RE), bounces over Stratford Broadway's famous cobblestones on 17th May 1968. Of note are the trolleybus traction standards used as street lighting columns, more than eight years after the trolleybuses had gone.

Three Green Line routes ran from Aldgate to the Grays and Tilbury area, the 723, 723A and 723B. These also converted from RT to Routemaster coach operation, initially intended to be RCL, but a restriction on the 723B meant RMCs had to be used. By 28th December 1971, when RMC1496 (GY) approaches East Ham Town Hall heading east, only the 723 remained and had mixed RMC and RCL operation. Four days later it converted to the ill-fated RC class operation.

Operated by Romford London Road Garage, route 721 linked Aldgate with Brentwood, and also had its RTs replaced by RCLs in 1965. On their last day of operation on the route, 31st December 1971, RCL2230 (RE) awaits departure from Aldgate, with an RMC on the 723 for company. Brand new RPs replaced them. These were not a success and in turn were ousted by new Leyland National "coaches" after couple of years. In turn, the unpopularity of the latter with passengers ensured the 721's demise.

The unreliability of the RCs on route 723 meant that RFs had to be used in the early/mid 1970s. On 3rd March 1974, downgraded modernised coach RF125 (GY) approaches Blackwall Tunnel along a remarkably deserted East India Dock Road. RFs were similarly used on the 721 covering for ailing RPs.

WEST END

Several of the cross-London Green Line routes passed through the West End, with some terminating within it. One was the 701 from Gravesend to Ascot, on which bus RF683(ST), still crew-operated, calls at Hyde Park Corner on 29th November 1967.

At Oxford Circus, where Green Line Coaches once had their headquarters above the Bakerloo Line tube station, modernised RF123 (DS) hurries through on the way from Luton to Dorking on 10th July 1970, still bearing its London Transport "bullseye" seven months after it became part of the London Country fleet.

Route 710, which had once linked Chesham and Amersham with Crawley was one of several Green Line routes which were curtailed or withdrawn in the late 1960s and early 1970s owing to declining patronage. On 19th February 1971, modernised RF172 (MA) heads along Bayswater Road towards Marble Arch bound for the route's revised eastern terminus at Baker Street. Not long afterwards, the 710 suffered an even more severe cut, running no further into Greater London than Uxbridge, and becoming more or less a glorified express bus route. It lasted only until October 1972 in this form.

Left: As referred to earlier, routes 715 and 715A were the first to convert from RF to RMC coach Routemasters. They were also the last to have them, and on their last day of operation, 28th April 1972, RMC1499 (GF) approaches St. Marylebone Church on its way from Hertford to Guildford.

Below: On 1st May 1973, RF46 (SA), a modernised Green Line coach downgraded to bus status, is stuck in traffic in Park Lane on its way from Dorking to Dunstable on route 712 owing to a May Day march protesting against Edward Heath's Tory regime. It appears to have lost its radiator filler cap!

A number of Green Line routes served Oxford Street, among them the 715 on which RF253 (HG), another modernised coach downgraded to bus status, has had to be pressed into service subbing for one of troublesome RPs on 30th May 1973. The famous Selfridges store forms an impressive backdrop.

Unreliability of the RPs (which had replaced RMCs on the 716 and 716A in March 1972) also saw the reappearance of RFs on these routes. On 29th February 1976, RF89 (WY) heads south along Park Lane on the 716A's long journey from Stevenage to Woking. The route was withdrawn the following May, effectively renumbered 716. The Leyland National coach on the right is probably one which has replaced RFs on other Green Line routes.

RFs were also called upon very late in the day to sub for newer types on route 705. On 19th April 1976, RF236 (DG) loads up at Hyde Park Corner bound from Windsor to Sevenoaks on the 705. It had been demoted from Green Line coach to Country bus status more than ten years previously.

Illustrating the revised dual-purpose livery given to the RPs later in life, RP44 (DS) passes the Royal Albert Hall on its way to Dorking on 22nd September 1979. By now, this route ventured no further north than Victoria.

As the system's name suggests, Country buses served many remote and rural locations in the countryside around London. On 3rd April 1972, RT4722 (LH) has just set off from Warlingham Park Hospital on route 408's long journey to Guildford. In September, this RT was one of the 34 sold back to London Transport, but only ran for them in red for a few weeks.

In rolling Hertforshie countryside, RT3135 (GR) is on its way from Harpenden to Luton on the long 321 on 13th July 1972. O.M.O. ANs took over this route next day.

I took this unusual view of RT1044 (HH) working route 312 from the front of an RF on route 706 heading through the village of Bourne End on 4th October 1972. The other RT ahead of us is on route 301.

The vast Epping Forest was crossed by a number of both Central and Country Area routes. On 31st May 1973, RT2504 (HA) passes through it on route 339 near the famous North Weald Airfield, an important base for R.A.F. fighters during the Battle of Britain. If we had been invaded in 1940, the Nazis planned to build a concentration camp for "undesirables" in nearby Thornwood Common.

On 30th March 1974, RML2425 (GR) heads for Uxbridge through rural scenery in Green Lane, Northwood, on the north-western fringes of the Central Area. Still in Lincoln Green livery, this was unfortunately one of the RMLs that fell foul of the vehicles spares shortage and never ran again. It was scrapped at the end of 1977.

Back in Epping Forest, modernised RF99 (ST) stands in for an RP on route 718's long journey from Windsor to Harlow when heading along Goldings Hill between Loughton and The Wake Arms on 31st March 1974.

Standing in for Garston's defunct RMLs, RTs virtually repossessed routes 306 and 311 in the winter of 1975/76. One of them, RT2779 (GR) heads along Radlett Lane on its way to Leavesden on 6th November 1975.

A year later, also in rural Hertfordshire, RMC1489 (SA) passes through the village of Smallford shortly before route 330's conversion to O.P.O. with Leyland Nationals. Within a few weeks, it had returned to London Transport for use as a trainer.

Routes 452 (formerly 457A) and 457 skirted the Central Area through rural scenery too. On 30th August 1979, RML2411 (WR) heads through the village of Iver on its way from Windsor to Uxbridge. Of note is the typical London Transport Country Area compulsory bus stop, still with its original flag nearly ten years after the LT/LCBS split.

London Country's last RF, modernised Green Line RF202 (DS), was operated during the summers of 1979 and 1980 on Ramblers Bus 418, which linked Sevenoaks Bus Station with a number of scenic Kentish villages. On 24th August 1980 it heads along the country lanes near Ide Hill. As may be observed it has been restored to 1967 Green Line livery, as was retained as a special events vehicle in this guise.

In the early 1980s, a new Green Line route 712 was introduced replacing parts of Country Bus route 339 and Central Bus route 247 (formerly 250) between Harlow, Epping and Romford. This ran through pleasant countryside, typified by that at Passingford Bridge, where RP2 (HA) passes The Rabbits pub on 20th July 1982.

CREW CHANGE

Left: Many buses, then as now, changed crews on the road at the point most convenient to their garages. On 10th September 1966, RF653 (HG) changes drivers in Ware Road, Hertford near to its garage in Fairfax Road, which was situated between this main road and the Great Eastern Hertford East railway line.

Below: Several garages were located actually on main roads that their buses served, therefore they changed crews outside them. This is so on 27th April 1968, as former Green Line RF242 (SA) changes drivers outside St. Albans Garage.

On 13th July 1968, RT2208 (GR) awaits its crew on St. Albans Road, Gartson opposite its garage on local route 318. This RT was one of the formerly red ones overhauled with RT3/1 bodies in 1963/64 to replace Country Area roofbox RTs. It ended its days as a trainer.

Adorned in N.B.C. corporate livery, RF640 (MA) awaits its driver in the lay-by opposite Amersham Garage when working short on route 359. For several years, this route between Amersham and Aylesbury was jointly operated between London Transport and United Counties, and it was not allowed to use Green Rover tickets on it.

The N.B.C. livery on RMC1473 (CM) is starting to fade as it awaits its crew outside Chelsham Garage on the last leg of route 403's journey from Wallington Station to Warlingham Park Hospital on 1st June 1977. An RCL recently arrived there from Grays is visible in the garage yard.

In their last couple of years working route 480 from Northfleet Garage, its RMLs displayed many different shades of green. Some had received N.B.C. corporate livery, but others like RML2342 (NF) retained their original Lincoln green with cream waistbands, which faded or peeled off altogether and contrasted with new panels in the original shade! It changes crew opposite Northfleet Garage on 4th March 1978.

EXPERIMENTAL

Throughout the life of London Transport's Country Area, and also London Country, a number of experimental vehicles were operated. One of the most obvious types was the 14-strong RC class of Willowbrook-bodied A.E.C. Reliances which operated on Green Line 705 for exactly two years after introduction in late November 1965, shared between Dunton Green and Windsor Garages. They had a striking grey livery with a broad dark green waistband, and ran an express service between Victoria and Windsor. On 11th July 1967, RC2 (DG) calls at Hyde Park Corner on its way south. After removal from this route, they were repainted in the same two-tone green livery as the modernised RFs and tried on various other Green Line routes. However despite the similar RP class being ordered for such use, they were not a success and ended up for a couple of years as Country buses in the mid-1970s before early withdrawal.

The first production MB-class A.E.C. Merlins to enter service (barring one solitary example on Red Arrow service) were eleven at Reigate Garage on local route 447 in March 1968, this route being chosen for trials as it was close to the Country Area's headquarters. With a very crammed front blind, brand new MB81 (RG) loads up in Bell Street, Reigate on 16th March 1968. Unfortunately, their smart appearance in Lincoln green with canary yellow waistbands belied their unreliability.

Other 1960s experimental types which served Reigate in the late 1960s were the XA and XF class front entrance double-deckers. Both with similar Park Royal bodywork, the eight XFs were Country Area Daimler Fleetlines sent to East Grinstead Garage for route 424, whilst the fifty XAs were red Leyland Atlanteans initially used on Central Area routes 24 and 67, and then the 271 and 76. Comparative trials were held between the latter and RMLs, but also eight of the XAs (which had been based at Stamford Hill Garage already) were swapped with the XFs for trials, resulting in these being used, still in red, on route 424. Also in Bell Street, Reigate, XA14 loads up on the 424 on 9th May 1968.

Probably the best-known Country Area experimental vehicle operating in the period covered by this book is prototype Green Line coach Routemaster RMC4. Originally numbered CRL4, it had a Leyland engine and, uniquely for a Routemaster, E.C.W. bodywork. After working various Green Line services, it eventually settled down at Hatfield Garage, from which it passes through Panshanger on route 716A on 21st July 1968. By now it has been modified to have the standard bonnet and headlamp arrangement given the 68 production RMCs, but retains its original non-opening upper-deck front windows. This historic Routemaster was the last in London Country's fleet, and is today part of the London Bus Company's Heritage Fleet with its original bonnet restored.

Eventually, the eight XFs returned to East Grinstead (where for a while three XAs were allocated, painted green and passed to London Country) and lasted the standard length of time for "provincial" vehicles, around 14-15 years. All of the XAs, including the three L.C.B.S. ones, were exported to Hong Kong early in early 1973. In full N.B.C. corporate livery, XF3 (EG) proceeds along Smallfield Road, Horley on 24th May 1979. This one had been experimentally fitted with a Cummins engine, between 1967 and 1975, and would be the last in service, withdrawn at the end of 1981. It was also the last ex-London Transport vehicle in normal service with London Country, and is now preserved.

BUS STATIONS

A number of purpose-built bus stations existed in the Country Area, as well as being served by Country buses and Green Line coaches in the Central Area. A good example was that at West Croydon, opened in January 1964 and forming a hub for a number of Country routes radiating southwards as well as catering for Central Area routes from other parts of the metropolis, including as far away as distant Chalk Farm. It was unique in having nameboards in the same style as Underground stations, one of which is visible in this view of RT4782 (CY) awaiting departure for distant Horsham in the pouring rain on 29th September 1967. The rain is so heavy that the RT is reflected in it on the road service! Both the RT and the Godstone RML behind (RML2307) ended their days as red buses.

A number of Green Line services called at the small Hammersmith, Butterwick Bus Station, and some terminated there. Modernised RF259 (NF) does so working route 701 on a dismal 27th December 1967. The large building on the right was Hammersmith Trolleybus Depot, used after the trolleys' withdrawal in 1960 until late 1966 to house the British European Airways' coach fleet, which London Transport operated and maintained.

A very well-known Country Area bus station was that at Hertford, situated between the Market Place and the River Lea. On 5th April 1968, two young bus spotters avidly note down the number of GS55 (HG) - I wonder if they will see this book, all these years later! By now, few GSs were still in service though Hertford still had a handful. They were not actually needed on route 308, which was also worked by RFs. Today, a modern shopping centre occupies this site with a small bus station attached to it. Vintage bus running days, featuring 1950s GSs, RFs and RTs are staged there nowadays, but the scenery bears no resemblance at all to that shown in this picture!

Another famous Country Area bus station is that at Stevenage, in the centre of the New Town which grew up in the early postwar years. On 27th April 1968, RT931 (SV) - yet another of the ex-red RT3/1-bodied vehicles - calls there on Broadwater loop route 800.

On the opposite side of London Transport's Country Area, Crawley New Town had a bus station too. Ex-coach RF220 (CY) arrives there on route 434 on 5th June 1968. This establishment, which was shared with Southdown, has been swept away, too.

Back at Hertford on 28th September 1968, another RT3/1, RT2807 (HG), awaits departure for Enfield on trunk route 310, remnants of which still exist today, but only going as far as Waltham Cross. Behind the RT are the bus station waiting rooms, offices and toilets which back on to the River Lea.

Above: At Uxbridge Bus Station, Central Area and Country Area routes terminated virtually end-on, alongside the Piccadilly and Metropolitan Lines' terminus. On 19th January 1969, RF631 (WR) lays over on route 458. The building on the left is the London Transport staff canteen, shared by bus and Underground staff alike. In the early 1980s, a new bus garage was built behind where the RF stands, and is still in use today.

Left: An impressive bus station was built in the 1930s for Country buses and Green Line coaches at Sevenoaks, and also served by Maidstone & District buses. On a rain-sodden 25th October 1968, ex-coach RF117 (DS) arrives there on route 413, which served local villages in the area. An RCL which has terminated on route 705 is just visible on the left. Alas, all this has been swept away now too.

A modern bus station existed at Hemel Hempstead, adjacent to the Marlowes Shopping Centre in the New Town. On a snowy 14th February 1969, a grubby RF695 (HH) awaits departure there on local route 344, which new MBSs will take over next day.

Down at Crawley again on 27th May 1970, ex-red RT3/1-bodied RT2814 (CY) lays over while working local route 476. Of note is the advert for Green Rovers on it, in the same style as the previous LT one but bearing the London Country "flying polo" logo.

A small bus and coach station existed in the forecourt of Dorking Garage, where RF643 (DS) stands working local route 439 on 27th May 1970. Of note is the unusual bus stop flag and lack of proper loading islands, as well as the very minute lettering on the RF's blind. Neither is conducive to today's "Health & Safety" regulations!

On the same day as the previous picture, RT4480 (GF) sets off from Guildford's Onslow Street Bus Station on local route 408A, which was also worked by RLHs. As the Dennis Loline on the left shows, this bus station was shared with Aldershot & District (by now a fellow N.B.C. company) as well as local independent operators Safeguard and Tillingbourne Valley. There was a second bus station adjacent to Guildford railway station, on the other side of the track of the main line. RT4480 was another to be bought back by London Transport in 1972.

Despite the appearance of MBSs there early in 1969, RFs were still very much part of the scene at Hemel Hempstead in the early 1970s. On 5th October 1972, RF629 (HH) is unusually working the 302, still then RT-operated, and about to run in to its garage from the bus station.

Several Green Line coach routes served the bus station adjacent to Golders Green Underground station. On 5th June 1973, RP32 (WY) calls there on its way from Chertsey to Hitchin on route 716. The bus station is little changed today, and has many coaches calling there on the National Express network.

Harlow New Town has its bus station, too, at which ex-coach RF243 (HG) arrives on 7th June 1974 on route 393 from Hertford with a monstrous concrete multi-storey car park as a backdrop.

By this period, Stevenage Bus Station had changed little, but most of its RTs had gone and some of the RFs still serving it carried N.B.C. Corporate livery. RF310 (HA) illustrates this when awaiting departure for Hertford, Harlow and Sawbridgeworth on route 390 on 16th July 1974, a route theoretically operated at the time by the ill-fated RCs.

Towards the close of London Country's operation of ex-London Transport types, a new bus station was opened at Grays, adjacent to the railway station and close to the London Country garage. On 15th September 1978, RCL2251 (GY), still in Lincoln Green livery and one of the last remaining there, sets off on local route 323. Behind it is an Eastern National Leyland National, identical to those being delivered to London Country at this time.

A monstrous creation known as the Brunel Bus Station and multi-storey car park was also built in Slough around this period, from which RML2348 (WR) departs on local route 407 on 19th May 1979. This would be the Country RMLs' last regularly-worked route early in 1980.

BANK HOLIDAY & SPECIAL EVENTS EXTRAS

For many years, extra Green Line coaches were run at Bank Holiday weekends, often ordinary service buses bearing blinds proclaiming them to be "Green Line Relief". However, at Whitsun weekend on 29th May 1967, RT979 (WR), one of the RTs painted in Green Line livery for relief duties, carries normal Green Line blinds when heading along Buckingham Palace Road, Victoria.

Country Area bus routes also worked extras for sporting events, the most well-known instance being special route 406F linking Epsom Station with the racecourse on Epsom Downs. On Derby Day 1967, an inspector directs passengers outside the station on to a line of RTs, headed by RT2499 (EG).

Saturday 30th September 1967 was not on a Bank Holiday weekend, but for some reason RT3508 (ST) is working a Green Line Relief journey on route 701 up to Victoria when heading along Chiswick High Road.

Smartly turned-out Green Line Relief RT1021 (NF) is amongst a line of RTs at the Epsom Downs terminus of the 406F which have brought spectators to The Derby from the station on 29th May 1968.

For some reason, "August" Bank Holiday Monday fell on 2nd September in 1968! On that day, RT3751 (SA) calls at Golders Green Station on a Green Line Relief journey on route 713, which a queue of passengers are boarding.

Resplendent in the new London Country livery of Lincoln green with yellow waistband, stock-numbers and fleet-names, RT3183 (WY) approaches Hampton Court Station on a Relief journey on route 716A up to London from Woking on Bank Holiday Monday 31st August 1971. This RT was subsequently preserved.

Green Line Reliefs on route 719 were also operated for race meetings at Brands Hatch, from where RT3145 (SJ), also recently given the new livery, departs after depositing its passengers on Easter Monday 3rd April 1972. Oddly, it shows the destination "West Kingsdown" which is in fact further south than this point.

Victoria was the place to be on Bank Holiday weekends to observe Green Line Relief workings, many of which terminated there. Also on Easter Monday 1972, RML2452 (NF) takes day trippers homewards to Gravesend in the evening. Owing to a one-way system implemented late in 1965, southbound coaches had to stop, as here, in Buckingham Palace Road rather than on Eccleston Bridge.

By Easter 1974, Leyland Nationals had begun to replace RFs on Green Line routes, and one of these approaches Eccleston Bridge as RT3130 (TG) lays over before returning to Tring on a 706 Green Line Relief journey. A primitive handwritten sign in its via blind box announces it as such.

Right: The Whitsun weekend of 1974 also saw plenty of activity at Victoria. On 27th May, RML2459 (WR) arrives with a 704 Relief journey. This was one of those that fell victim to the spares shortage, being delicensed in June 1974. It never ran again and was scrapped at the end of 1977. Of note is the London Transport Green Line "bullseye" symbol still on the wall on the corner of Eccleston Bridge on the right, with maps and details of Green Line services beneath it.

Below: Presumably subbing for one of the unfortunate RPs, E.C.W.-bodied Bristol LH BN5 (DG) is not really on a "Relief" journey of the 705 when crossing Lambeth Bridge on 3rd September 1975. Both London Transport and London Country bought vehicles of this type in the mid-1970s to replace their ageing RFs. They lasted nowhere near as long as them though!

The Biggin Hill Air Displays also warranted extra bus services, mostly on route 410 between Bromley North Station and the Airfield. On 20th September 1975, RT4742 (RG) brings spectators homewards at Keston Mark Inn, passing two coach Routemasters going to collect more of them.

On 19th May 1976, RMC1493 (SJ) turns from Buckingham Palace Road onto Elizabeth Bridge, Victoria on 719 Relief journey to Brands Hatch. RMCs had operated route 719 when new, but it only ran north of Victoria at the time.

Derby Day 1st June 1977 was the last one at which ex-London Transport vehicles operated route 406F in any numbers. RML2340 (NF) loads up outside Epsom Station, with RCL2238, which oddly claims to be on a "Special Railway Service" following.

Owing to a rail strike on 20th July 1982, many ordinary London Country service buses worked Green Line Reliefs. Complete with "Watfordwide" route branding, Atlantean AN160 (GR) heads out of Victoria along Grosvenor Place.

In evening rush hour traffic passing Kensington Gardens, RP14 (WY) operates a Relief journey on new Green Line route 730, probably to Woking on 24th June 1983. It was withdrawn two months later, the last of the class following early in 1984.

ESSEX

This section of the book looks briefly at places in the Home Counties served by London Transport Country Area/London Country buses and Green Line coaches, starting with Essex and going clockwise around London. The only major centres of their operation in Essex were Harlow and Grays, the county in fact also being served by Central Area red buses based at Loughton. On 27th June 1965, Green Line RT4507 (GY) stands at the Tilbury Ferry terminus of route 723, shortly before being replaced by new RCL coach Routemasters.

On 29th September 1968, RT3498 (GY) approaches Grays War Memorial on local route 328. Grays Garage had been opened in 1936, and was enlarged in the early post-war years after a number of local Eastern National routes in the area were transferred to London Transport.

The Essex market town of Epping also had a Country Area garage which was opened in 1934, but it was closed in 1963 and replaced by a new one in Harlow New Town. Epping was also served by Central Area (red) bus routes in the 20 group and the 250 (later replaced by the 247) for many years. On 3rd May 1969, Green Line Relief RT635 (HA) turns from Epping High Street into Station Road on route 339's double-run through the town serving the Central Line station.

Brentwood was a "border town" between the London Transport/ London Country and Eastern National operating areas, also served by Central Area routes such as the 247 and 287 when RT4491 (HA) calls at the High Street stop on 29th May 1970. Route 339 continued to Warley, from where anyone wanting to travel to be Grays area by bus would have to use Eastern National services, as there was no LT Country Area or London Country link between the two areas.

Epping Forest occupies a large chunk of the former Country Area in south-west Essex. On 27th September 1973, RP74 (HA) speeds through it near Buckhurst Hill, unusually curtailed at Stratford Broadway on Green Line route 720.

With a very badly-set destination blind, RT2504 (HA) arrives at Epping Station on 26th September 1974 on a rush hour journey of route 396, which travelled through inner west Essex and over the border into Hertfordshire, terminating at Bishops Stortford, one of the Country Area's furthest outposts.

Back in the Grays area, RCL2248 (GY) calls at the rather bleak Tilbury Civic Square working trunk route 370 to Romford. In common with many RCLs originally based at Grays for Green Line service, in later years it worked there as a London Country bus. The class would have a brief resurrection in the early 1980s as red London Transport buses.

A number of bus routes operated in the Grays and Tilbury area for the benefit of the many industries there. In the evening rush hour of 1st April 1976, RMC1507 (GY) awaits departure from the East Purfleet Thames Board Mills terminus of one such route, the 375. This RMC was briefly used as a trainer by London Transport when sold back to them, but then sold privately for preservation. It is smartly restored to 1962 Green Line livery today in the London Bus Company's Heritage Fleet.

On the same day, RMC1470 (GY) passes through the drab scenery of Arisdale Avenue in South Ockendon on route 369, another which served the industrial establishments in this part of south-west Essex.

KENT

Across the Thames in north-west Kent, the Country Area had a larger share of local bus services, with bus garages at Dartford, Dunton Green, Northfleet and Swanley and a small Green Line coach garage at Tunbridge Wells. On 2nd May 1968, RT2874 (SJ) - one of the ex-red RTs with RT3/1 bodies - has just called at Swanley Junction Station and is running in to the nearby garage.

Gravesend was another "border town", where Country Area buses and Green Line coaches met Maidstone and District buses, which had a garage in the town and operated services to the east of it. On 5th March 1969, ex-coach RF220 (NF) sets off from the Gravesend terminus of local route 490, heading for the village of Hartley Court. Of note is its open filler cap, which is neatly included in the front "bullseye" symbol.

Also in Gravesend the same day, a well-loaded RT4745 (NF) heads along New Road on local route 487. New O.M.O. MBSs replaced RTs on several such services here shortly afterwards.

Running around the block at the Gravesend Clocktower terminus on route 489 also on 5th March 1969, GS54 (NF) is one of a handful based at Northfleet Garage which shared routes such as the 489 and 490 with RFs, running to villages south of the town.

Further south within Kent, Sevenoaks Bus Station was a hub serving several Country Area routes, as well as some Maidstone & District services which went beyond their area. These were operated from nearby Dunton Green Garage, whose RT3530 (DG) calls there on a very wet 25th October 1969, working route 454 which linked Tonbridge and Chipstead.

On the same occasion RF582 (DG) arrives at Sevenoaks Bus Station working local route 404 which served Shoreham Village and, like the 454, the curiously-named Southern Region Bat & Ball Station.

Although close to the Central Area and in fact served by red bus route 96 (which had been the 696 trolleybus and the 96 tram before that), the Country Area bus garage in Dartford had been taken over, along with local services, from Maidstone & District by the L.P.T.B. in 1933. A number of routes terminated there, as did short workings on route 480, on which RML2345 (NF) departs on 18th July 1974. This RML fell victim to the spares shortage in March 1975, and after removal to storage at Grays Garage, was progressively cannibalised until it was little more than a skeletal hulk four years later. However, unlike seventeen other less-cannibalised RMLs which went for scrap, it was rescued by London Transport and effectively reconstructed at Aldenham Works, re-entering service in May 1981 as a red bus, remaining in service until July 2005!

On the same day, RMC1462 (DT) descends East Hill into Dartford town centre on local route 499, which would later be operated by Maidstone Corporation Leyland PD2s, as illustrated earlier.

At the foot of the hill, RML2328 (NF) passes some quaint old buildings in Lowfield Street in Dartford town centre, and is about to cross the bridge over the River Darenth. By this time, the 480 continued beyond its earlier Denton terminus east of Gravesend to Valley Drive, a new housing development which was the furthest east in Kent that London Country vehicles reached.

The 480 was the last major London Country route to be RML operated, finally succumbing to O.P.O. late in 1979. In their last couple of years, some of the RMLs became very shabby indeed. One of these, RML2325 (NF) calls at The Railway Inn in Greenhithe on 4th March 1978. All of the 480's last RMLs passed back to London Transport, remaining in service until 2003-2005.

Modernised Green Line RF202 (NF) was the last of all the London Transport and London Country RFs to remain in normal service. On 24th May 1979, it passes through the Kentish village of Hartley on the way from Gravesend to New Ash Green.

Not only did the last major London Country route operating RMLs serve Dartford, so did the last using RMCs, the 477, which retained them until January 1980. On 1st October 1979, RMC1512 (SJ) is pursued along Market Street, Dartford by a new Leyland National. This RMC would be the last RMC of all in London Country use five months later.

Some of the last SMs operated in the Dartford Area, too. One of those which received N.B.C. Corporate livery, SM458 (DT) approaches Dartford Market Place also on 1st October 1979, on route 499 where they had replaced RMCs. By the end of 1981, all of this unfortunate class had perished.

SUSSEX

The extreme southern edge of the Country Area reached into Sussex, where the towns of Crawley and East Grinstead had London Transport garages, both of which were inherited from the East Surrey company. On 5th June 1968, the driver of smart RF569 (CY) makes up his waybill after arrival at Crawley Bus Station.

Route 409 penetrated into Southdown territory beyond East Grinstead, as far as Forest Row, and originally Green Rover tickets could not be used on that section of route. On 27/5/70, RT940 (GD) is actually on loan to Godstone Garage when subbing for an RML on the 409 in East Grinstead High Street.

The southernmost point of all reached by Country Area and London Country buses was Horsham in Sussex, which had the benefit of two trunk routes which came all the way from Croydon, the 405 via Crawley and the 414 via Dorking. Also on 27th May 1970, RT3124 (DS) arrives at the Horsham, Carfax terminus. Both of these busy routes converted to RCL operation in the spring of 1972. Today, the 405 survives as a London Buses route, but runs only as far south as Redhill.

SURREY

Much of Surrey, including all of its eastern part, was served by the Country Area which in fact had inherited the Easy Surrey operations (latterly part of London General Country Services) including its headquarters and garage in Reigate. Other garages in the county were at Chelsham, Dorking, Godstone, Guildford, Leatherhead and Addlestone. On 6th May 1967, RLH25 (WY) from the latter garage arrives at Woking Station on route 436A, one of several routes in the area that needed this type owing to the number of low railway bridges on the former London & South Western system.

A route that did not need RLHs, yet occasionally was operated by them, was the 420 between Woking and the Sheerwater Estate. Also on 6th May 1967, RT4752 (WY) sets off from Woking Station.

Reigate was the heart of Country bus operation in Surrey. On 16th March 1968, RT3203 (RG) approaches Reigate Garage in Bell Street on the busy 406. This became the headquarters of the new London Country outfit on 1st January 1970. This RT was one of the 34 sold back to London Transport in 1972.

Many of the routes operated by Addlestone Garage converged at the crossroads by the nearby Dukes Head pub. On 9th May 1968, RF651 (WY) has just set off on a short working of the 456 to the village of Maybury.

Also in Addlestone that day, RLH46 (GF) approaches the level crossing at Addlestone Station, working route 463 to Walton-On-Thames, which was shared between Addlestone and Guildford Garages.

9th May 1968 is also the date of this picture of RT4407 (LH) passing through Epsom town centre, on route 418, which linked Bookham with Kingston and, curiously, had roads well within the Central Area near Tolworth all to itself.

Surrey's county town, Guildford, was served both by London Transport Country Area/London Country buses and those of Aldershot & District. On 27th May 1970, RT2809 (GF) arrives at its Onslow Street Bus Station working route 415, with blinds already showing its next destination, Ripley.

Back in Epsom High Street, downgraded modernised RF213 (LH) terminates on local route 481. Of note are the two traditional London Transport bus stops, the one furthest from the camera is an old metal L.G.O.C. one

Another modernised Green Line RF, RF140 (WY) is still in Green Line livery on 16th July 1975, but working as a bus on the 462, which linked Addlestone with Leatherhead. It passes through Church Cobham and interestingly has upper case via points on its blind.

On the last day of Green Line route 716's operation to Chertsey, 13th May 1976, RP28 (SV) passes the Dukes Head at Addlestone. Following the withdrawal of this working, the 716A to Weybridge was renumbered 716.

The Surrey town of Caterham-On-The Hill was served by both red and green London buses. On 1st June 1977, RT1018 (CM), one of the three painted in N.B.C. corporate green livery, terminates there on local route 453.

The Thameside town of Staines had been in the Country of Middlesex prior to its abolition on 1st April 1965, but instead of being incorporated into Greater London as most of the rest of Middlesex was, it became part of Surrey! This town also had a Country bus garage, from which local services, trunk routes and Green Line coaches operated. On 26th September 1977, RML2442 (ST) heads along South Street in the town centre on route 441, whose full route ran from Staines to High Wycombe.

BERKSHIRE

Country Area buses served the Berkshire towns of Slough and Windsor. On 1st June 1968, RT1086 (MA) passes through Slough town centre on the long 353, which started at Windsor and ventured further out into Buckinghamshire, serving Amersham and Chesham, before terminating at Berkhamsted in Hertfordshire.

Similarly, route 335 was a long cross-country service, linking Windsor and Watford. Also in Slough town centre on 1st June 1968, RT4563 (GR) is running in to Garston Garage.

Local services in the Slough Area were operated by Windsor Garage. RML2459 (WR) lays over outside it while working the 417, also on 1st June 1968. This is one of the seventeen RMLs which expired during the mid-1970s spare parts shortage, and was never to run again.

RML2436 (WR) was another of the Country RMLs which perished. On 8th March 1969, it heads west out of Slough town centre on local route 484, followed by a Thames Valley Bristol Lodekka typical of those heading for such towns as Maidenhead and Reading.

BUCKINGHAMSHIRE

As mentioned earlier, the Country Area included the south-eastern tip of Buckinghamshire, serving Amersham, Chesham, High Wycombe and Aylesbury. On 29th June 1968, RT3335 (MA) sets off from Chesham Broadway on its long trip to Windsor on route 353.

On the same day as the previous picture, RF293 (MA) arrives in Chesham on local route 348B. Originally a Central Area red bus, this had been converted to a Green Line coach in 1956, and then became a Country Area green bus upon overhaul ten years later. It retains its brackets for the Green line side-boards.

High Wycombe had both a Country Area/London Country bus garage, and one for Thames Valley who operated services to the west and south-west of the town. On 28th September 1968, Green Line "Relief" RT620 (MA) sets off on route 362 bound for the village of Ley Hill.

A network of Country Area routes was based upon Amersham Garage. On 14th September 1974, RF561 (MA) approaches Amersham Station bound for, as its blind says, "High Wycombe London Country Garage" on route 364, which had been renumbered from 362A. This was to enable newer vehicles with three-track number blinds to operate it; inevitably the RF has had to sub for one of them.

Also at Amersham Station, and having just passed beneath the bridge beyond which the Metropolitan Line's trains run into their terminal sidings, RF675 (MA) heads for Chesham on route 336, which ran from Watford to Chesham and had until the mid-1960s been operated by RLHs.

BEDFORDSHIRE

The southern tip of Bedfordshire was also served by London Transport's Country Area and London Country, around Dunstable and Luton. At the latter's Park Square, ex-coach RF238 (LS) loads up for a trip to Kensworth on local route 364A on 28th September 1968.

At the same spot as the previous picture, RF55 (LS), another ex-coach, sets off on route 366, a limited stop service which had replaced the Luton to Welwyn Garden City railway line in 1965.

At Park Square on the same day, RT3246 (LS) works one of the double-deck journeys on the old route 364 between Luton and Flamstead Village. The rest of the 364 and 364A east of Luton to Hitchin was the preserve of RFs, serving some very narrow country lanes. Both routes were withdrawn in 1973 and taken over by independent operator Court Line, which however did not last very long.

Route 321 was the major Country Area trunk route that served Luton, running all the way to Uxbridge via St. Albans and Watford, although most journeys from there terminated at either Maple Cross or Rickmansworth, as RT3135 (GR) is doing on 13th July 1972, the route's last day of crew operation. It contrasts with a United Counties Bristol Lodekka at the Park Square terminus.

By this time, the Flamstead Village section of route 364 was also operated by RFs. RF625 (LS) stands on the other side of Park Square. The small Luton Garage was in Park Street West, just around the corner.

HERTFORDSHIRE

The bulk of Hertfordshire was served by the LT Country Area, with garages at Tring, Hemel Hempstead (Two Waters), Garston (North Watford), St. Albans, Hatfield, Stevenage and Hertford at the time the survey in this book commences. The latter was a veritable hub of services radiating throughout most of the county. On 30th March 1968, RF633 (HG) sets of from Hertford Bus Station on route 331 for Buntingford, one of the furthest extremities reached.

Hatfield's original bus garage was replaced in 1959 by a new one, and on 27th April 1968, RT3207 (HF) passes between the two of them on a short working of trunk route 303 to Hatfield Station. It would be one of the 34 green RTs sold back to London Transport in 1972.

A small garage at Tring provided buses for the busy Country bus route 301, which ran all the way from Little Bushey and Watford to Aylesbury, Green Line coach routes 706 and 707 which paralleled it along the A41 from Aylebsury to Watford before crossing Central London and ending up in the distant Surrey hills, as well as some local bus routes. On 29th June 1968, RT2700 (TG) changes crew opposite the garage. It is an ex-red RT3/1-bodied vehicle due at that time for withdrawal.

One of Tring's local routes was the 394, on which RF302 (MA) arrives at the garage on the same day. It had been converted from a Country bus to a Green Line coach in 1956, and renumbered from RF521. However, when downgraded back to bus status ten years later it was not renumbered!

St. Peters Street, St. Albans, the city's main shopping street, is quiet on Sunday, 18th August 1968, as RT2999 (SA), another RT3/1, passes through on local route 325. The unusual blind display is of note; fellow local route 354 had a similar one, too.

The garage named Hemel Hempstead was actually on the A41 at Two Waters, and on 4th October 1972, modernised Green Line RF75 (EG) runs in to it for the driver's meal relief after its long journey from East Grinstead to the new town's bus station on route 708.

On the borders between the Central and Country Areas, Cuffley in Hertfordshire was served by red bus route 242 and green bus routes 308 and 308A when ex-coach RF286 (HG) climbs out of the town to run through the country lanes to Hertford on 21st March 1973. Today, the 242 still runs operated by Potters Bar Garage, but is no longer a London Buses service.

On 26th April 1973, modernised RF245 (HG) is still in Green Line livery when departing from Hertford Bus Station on route 390, which meandered its way across the Hertfordshire countryside from Stevenage to Hertford and Harlow, ending up in the Essex town of Sawbridgeworth. The masked blind display is necessary to accommodate destination displays for a large number of routes operated from Hertford Garage.

Modernised Green Line RF140 (WY) is a long way from home when calling at Stevenage New Town's 1950s Bus Station when deputising for one of the troublesome RPs, then only two years old, on the long 716 from Chertsey to Hitchin on 16th July 1974.

By 30th April 1975, the long trunk route 301 had gained RMCs, though it never converted from RT to them completely. RMC1513 (HH) heads along The Avenue, Bushey nearing its southern terminus. Many years later, this RMC (having been returned in the meantime to LT and used as a trainer) would be one of those resurrected for the X15 Docklands Express.

At this period, RTs and RMCs at Two Waters Garage were intermixed between the 301 and 302, and various local routes serving Hemel Hempstead New Town. On the same day as the previous picture, RT3898 (HH) approaches its home garage, with a very uninformative blind display.

In common with several other traditional Green Line routes by this time, the 715 had been split into two sections, no longer crossing Central London. Its northern section, running from Hertford to Oxford Circus was renumbered 735. This did not last long, and on 17th May 1980, RP13 (HG) passes through the centre of Hertford. By now, the RPs, delivered only in 1971/72, were on the way out, too.